# BFI FILM CLASSICS

. . . . . . . . . . . . . . . . . . . . . . . . . .

## Edward Buscombe
SERIES EDITOR

## Colin MacCabe and David Meeker
SERIES CONSULTANTS

Cinema is a fragile medium. Many of the great classic films of the past now exist, if at all, in damaged or incomplete prints. Concerned about the deterioration in the physical state of our film heritage, the National Film and Television Archive, a Division of the British Film Institute, has compiled a list of 360 key films in the history of the cinema. The long-term goal of the Archive is to build a collection of perfect show-prints of these films, which will then be screened regularly at the Museum of the Moving Image in London in a year-round repertory.

BFI Film Classics is a series of books commissioned to stand alongside these titles. Authors, including film critics and scholars, film-makers, novelists, historians and those distinguished in the arts, have been invited to write on a film of their choice, drawn from the Archive's list. Each volume presents the author's own insights into the chosen film, together with a brief production history and a detailed filmography, notes and bibliography. The numerous illustrations have been specially made from the Archive's own prints.

With new titles published each year, the BFI Film Classics series will rapidly grow into an authoritative and highly readable guide to the great films of world cinema.

Could scarcely be improved upon ... informative, intelligent, jargon-free companions.
*The Observer*

Cannily but elegantly packaged BFI Classics will make for a neat addition to the most discerning shelves.
*New Statesman & Society*

Alexander Korda and H. G. Wells examine the designs for *Things to Come*

BFI FILM CLASSICS

# THINGS TO COME

......................

*Christopher Frayling*

BRITISH FILM INSTITUTE

*bfi*

BFI PUBLISHING

First published in 1995 by the
BRITISH FILM INSTITUTE
21 Stephen Street, London W1P 2LN

The British Film Institute exists
to promote appreciation, enjoyment, protection and
development of moving image culture in and throughout
the whole of the United Kingdom.
Its activities include the National Film and
Television Archive; the National Film Theatre;
the Museum of the Moving Image;
the London Film Festival; the production and
distribution of film and video; funding and
support for regional activities;
Library and Information Services;
Stills, Posters and Designs; Research,
Publishing and Education; and the monthly
*Sight and Sound* magazine.

British Library Cataloguing in Publication Data
A catalogue record for this book is available from the British Library

ISBN 0–85170–480–8

The film *Things to Come* is available from CTE (Carlton) Ltd for
exploitation throughout the world excluding North America and The
Sam Goldwyn Company for exploitation in North America. CTE
(Carlton) Ltd – Tel: 0171 224 3339. The Sam Goldwyn Company –
Tel: 0101 310 552 2255.

Designed by
Andrew Barron & Collis Clements Associates

Typesetting by
Fakenham Photosetting Limited, Norfolk

Printed in Great Britain by
The Trinity Press, Worcester

# CONTENTS

· · · · · · · · · · · · · · · · · · · · · · · ·

## ACKNOWLEDGMENTS

My thanks are due to Tony Aldgate, Tim Benton, Bernard Myers, Gillian Naylor, David Queensberry, Colin Sorenson, Penny Sparke, Moira Tait, and Helen Rees (then of the Design Museum) who asked me to deliver the first Paul Reilly Memorial Lecture, parts of which have been incorporated into this book. Also to the long-suffering staff at the National Art Library, the Royal College of Art Library and the BFI Library and Information Services. Ed Buscombe of the BFI was an equally long-suffering editor ('Is *Things to Come* coming soon?' he would ask), Sue Bobbermein provided research support, the Stills, Posters and Designs Department moved very fast, and Markku Salmi did wonders with the credits. Elaine Burrows of the National Film and Television Archive helped to establish the film's original running time. Gill Plummer and Helen Frayling managed somehow, and under pressurised conditions, to decipher my handwriting. The University of Illinois Research and Reference Centre (H. G. Wells archive) kindly supplied the typescript letters from Wells to Arthur Bliss.

    *Things to Come* is unusual, in that H. G. Wells' original treatment (entitled *Whither Mankind?*), his shooting script *and* release script have all been published – the shooting script at the time (as *Things to Come – a film story*), the treatment and release script in Leon Stover's *The Prophetic Soul*; the BFI also holds an original of the release script in its collections, which I checked against the published transcription. All scholars who work on *Things to Come* are indebted to Leon Stover's book, the commentary of which deals interestingly with H. G. Wells' social and political ideas in the mid-1930s. This book is more concerned with *Things to Come* as a film, or as a visual experience, and its intention is to provide another, congruent, way into this underrated classic. The book is dedicated to the RCA art and design students to whom I have lectured, on the subject of *Things to Come* and matters arising, for many years: their comments, and above all their *work*, have often proved an inspiration.

Professor Christopher Frayling
London, January 1995

(r. to l.) Ned Mann (special effects director), William Cameron Menzies (director) and Harry Zech (special effects photography)

# INTRODUCTION

....................

My experience of the film *Things to Come* began in autumn 1970, when I first heard – and was thrilled by – the suite of music which Arthur Bliss wrote for the soundtrack, at an orchestral concert in the Albert Hall. I was humming the *March* for days. A couple of years later, I saw the film itself on the big screen, in the Imperial War Museum's viewing theatre: I was researching and archiving RAF newsreels of the Second World War at the time, and, if memory serves, my invitation to watch the film – on a very cold Monday morning, together with three other people – was for the purposes of aircraft recognition. The 35 mm print of *Things to Come* not only warmed me up: forgive the cliché, but it sent shivers of a different sort up my spine as well. The music, the design, the special effects, the editing, the conviction of the performances – above all, the sheer *scale* and *ambition* of the film – made me forget all about whether or not Raymond Massey's bi-plane was a Hawker 1-SE, and how many Avro 504s were in Ralph Richardson's bedraggled fleet of old-fashioned crates, and where on earth the design for the twin-hulled Basra Bombers came from. So I had to ask the projectionist to run the film again, from the beginning of course, with the theatre's lights half on, to let me consult my government-issue silhouette book.

Sure, some of the acting creaked a little, and the characters tended to be arranged in tidy *tableaux vivants* as they addressed the audience rather than each other. But that didn't seem to matter. What mattered was that here was a British (well, Hungarian-British) science fiction movie which, like the best of predictive literature, had thought hard about the philosophy and politics of science as well as the hardware, the social structure of the future as well as the costumes. And it looked *great*. A whole universe away from the white zipper suits and steering wheels of Saturday morning serials. Up to then, I'd associated science fiction in the British media with Daleks which couldn't move upstairs, Thunderbird puppets, Nicholas Parsons in a metal helmet advertising Blue Car Travel, robotic Martians with shell-shaped heads discussing mashed potatoes, and a large white bubble chasing a man in a blazer across the sands at Portmeirion. There had been the television *Quatermass*, with its unforgettable image of an astronaut transmuting into a giant vegetable in the vaults of Westminster Abbey, but that was a long time ago. And there had been *2001: A Space Odyssey*, which I'd watched again and again from the front row of the London Casino, letting the 'beyond the infinite' sequence make me dizzy: but I *still* couldn't figure out why a four-million year-old minimalist sculpture, school of Donald Judd, was whizzing around the stratosphere and somehow distributing wisdom wherever it happened to land, and why Keir Dullea had turned into a starchild in a neo-Georgian hotel bedroom.

A visit to the 'Thirties' exhibition at the Hayward Gallery in autumn 1979 stimulated thoughts about the look of *Things to Come* – 1936 *and* 2036 – and how it connected with the domestic design of the period: everything from the transparent furniture and huge flowers in oversized vases to the interiors (which seemed vaguely to resemble some of the more glitzy 1930s hotel foyers and bathrooms) to the style of the graphics and the elaborate deco flying machines. Most of the visitors to the 'Thirties' show seemed to think this was all the stuff of nostalgia; but in 1936 it must have been – credibly – the shape of things to come. Then, a visit to the Institute of Contemporary Arts in January 1980 to see the Moholy-Nagy exhibition introduced me to sixteen stills of the Hungarian artist-designer's visual contributions to the 'building of Everytown' sequence from *Things to Come*, as well as to his abstract film *Light-play* (1930) – involving rays of light projected through a metal mobile sculpture, with superimpositions – which resembled moments from that sequence in Korda's epic. The exhibition did not speculate about Moholy's exact contribution to *Things to Come*, but another seed had been planted.

I have seen *Things to Come* many times since then. On the big screen, on video, on television in Alexander Korda seasons. The post-*Star Wars* generation of multi-million-dollar 'B' movies has, if anything, made the seriousness – the painful seriousness – of *Things to Come* all the more cherishable. Pauline Kael's famous judgment on these films – that they were part of a general 'infantilisation' of mainstream Hollywood in the late 1970s – is not a charge that could *ever* be levelled at Korda and H. G. Wells. I've even used the film for teaching on a course about design in the movies, at the Royal College of Art – exploring the evolution of 'the idea of the city' from the filmic symphonies of the 1920s (Walther Ruttmann's *Berlin*, Dziga Vertov's *Man with a Movie Camera*, Fritz Lang's *Metropolis* and Sergei Eisenstein's *October*) to the gloomy postmodernist fantasies of the 1980s (notably

Ridley Scott's *Blade Runner*, with its retro-Thirties Los Angeles in the year 2019 drenched with acid rain, Terry Gilliam's *Brazil* and Paul Verhoeven's *RoboCop*). Via, of course, William Cameron Menzies' *Things to Come*, the look of which is now an established part of the fantasy designer's lexicon – again, camp in retrospect (the film was regularly shown in the 1980s on American pay-tv in a season called *Summer Camp*), earnest at the time. And also via Alexander Mackendrick's *The Man in the White Suit* (1951), the 'fibre construction' sequence of which explicitly parodies *Things to Come*. At a design conference in Glasgow in September 1993, I was discussing *Things to Come* when Victor Papanek – guru of alternative/appropriate technology and author of *How Things Don't Work* – stood up and informed the audience that as a schoolboy he had appeared as an extra at Denham and shouted 'Here comes the Boss, here's to the Boss': a bizarre link between modernity according to H. G. Wells and its polar opposite.

While mainstream film histories have tended on the whole to patronise *Things to Come* – emphasising the wordy script to the exclusion of everything else, and never quite managing to forgive H. G. Wells for creating a utopia rather than the usual dystopia – and literary scholars have tended to adopt Wells' own disillusioned view of the experience of working on it – emphasising what they consider to be the element of 'lowest common denominator' brought to the project by the brothers Korda – *Things to Come* has for the last twenty years been a cult film on the art school circuit, and as such has entered the bloodstream of contemporary visual culture through the work of countless graphic, fashion and product designers. Maybe that's why I have remained so fond of it, even though the gaps in its politics – gender, ecology, small is beautiful, post-colonialism – have become ever more apparent with the passage of time.

The group who made the film were an explosive bunch: the short-fused Wells, the passionate Vincent Korda, the go-between Lajos Biró, the easygoing – but seriously rattled – William Cameron Menzies, the faintly bemused Arthur Bliss, and presiding over them the charming and plausible Alexander Korda, who seems to have realised too late the sheer immensity of what he had taken on – too late, that is, to do much about it. Out of the resulting combustion came a film which certainly bears the stamp of the strong personalities who contributed to it, and which pulls in several directions at once. A film which is also, in my view, one of the most significant British films ever made.

*Things to Come* is to Modernism as *Blade Runner* is to Postmodernism. Which is saying a lot.

# 1
........................
## THE SHAPE OF THINGS

When British cinemagoers first saw William Cameron Menzies' version of H. G. Wells' *Things to Come* in March 1936, they would also have seen – as part of the full supporting programme – an issue of the newsreel *March of Time* (British issue number 5) entitled *England's Hollywood*.

It began with shots of cloth-capped workers and aproned crasftsmen happily going through a gate and back to work. 'On the outskirts of London,' said the optimistic commentary, 'thousands of workers of various trades and callings find employment in what is the newest and most picturesque of British industries.' Over a sequence which showed elaborate film sets being constructed, the commentary went on: 'And here each time a camera turns, it is a manifestation of a British victory in conquering for England an industry and source of revenue which was almost entirely in foreign hands only a decade ago.' A fleet of gigantic black flying fortresses, powered by four propellers apiece and looking like streamlined Odeon cinemas in the sky, flew across the screen with a distinctive humming sound as the voice-over intoned: 'Today, even teaching Hollywood new tricks of production, as in Alexander Korda's *Things to Come*, England takes her share of the English-speaking market, for her producers are giving the public films that the Americans cannot supply. British films with proper British taste and British accents.'

Shots of black-shirted aviators looking down from a promenade deck and of Ralph Richardson in a tin hat – with a Tudor Rose emblem stuck onto it – watching the skies were followed by a sequence showing Korda's post-production team busily assembling a complete cut of the film. Then Alexander Korda himself, in tortoise-shell rimmed spectacles, seated at his executive desk, cigar in one hand, bound script of *Things to Come* in the other: 'Alexander Korda, director of London

Film Productions Limited, in 1932 founded his own company and the following year produced *The Private Life of Henry VIII.*' As Percy Grainger's well-known tune *Country Gardens* played softly in the background, the audience could see the component parts of Denham studios being put together: a large sound-stage, a board with 'Denham' painted on it, a back-lot, acres of scaffolding. 'At Denham, he is building with the backing of the Prudential Assurance Company and Sir Connaught Guthric what are reported to be England's largest studios.' Then over a shot of Alexander Korda, his younger brother Vincent (the film's 'designer of settings'), Georges Périnal (director of photography), William Cameron Menzies (director) and H. G. Wells – all standing, somewhat stiffly, behind a mahogany desk on which some paper designs for *Things to Come* were spread out – the commentary continued: 'Today, England's movie-makers approach their problem with imagination as well as money. And in their ranks is one of Great Britain's foremost imaginations. Voice to the future of British cinema is given by a British author of world renown –who has now given up writing books entirely in favour of the cinema, Mr H. G. Wells. Just back from inspecting America's Hollywood, as the guest of Charlie Chaplin.'

The 69-year-old Wells was wearing a pin-striped suit and a club tie; he looked tubby, his unregulated moustache was going grey and he had noticeable bags under his eyes, but his gift for rhetoric and distinctive, slightly Kentish and more than slightly squeaky voice – as heard on BBC radio broadcasts since 1929 – came over as memorably as ever. Plus his well-known ability to think in paragraphs. He wasn't reading a script, but sounded as though he was. 'At the present time,' he lectured to camera, 'there are great general interests which oppress men's minds – excite and interest them. There's the onset of war, there's the increase of power, there's the change of scale and the change of conditions in the world. And in one or two of our films here, we've been trying without any propaganda or pretension or preachment of any sort, we've been trying to work out some of those immense possibilities that appeal, we think, to everyman. We are attempting here the film of imaginative possibility. That, at any rate, is one of the challenges that we are going to make to our friends and rivals at Hollywood.' A montage of billboards being posted on Broadway for Korda's *The Private Life of Henry VIII* and *The Ghost Goes West* (both of which were showing in New York, in autumn 1935) accompanied the newsreel's final message: 'Eloquent proof of the British Hollywood's challenge to America's Hollywood are certain signs visible this winter in New York City ... no longer weak and crippled by foreign invasion, but now actually competing even on Broadway with the best films that any land can produce. TIME MARCHES ON.'

It must have seemed ironic to those who took the main feature seriously that this hymn of praise to national economic competition should accompany Wells' *Things to Come* – a polemic in favour of world economic planning and a New World Order where destructive trade wars and financial conflict would become things of the past. Ironic, too, that Wells had just returned from visiting his friend Charlie Chaplin in Hollywood (in late November 1935, while post-production was being completed on *Things to Come*), where he noted ruefully that Charlie was 'struggling with parallel difficulties to mine', which had turned him into 'a tired man'. For Chaplin was at that time putting the finishing touches to *Modern Times*, his satire on automation and the American system of manufacture – both of which were *models* for Wells' vision of the future. Wells had recently visited Joseph Stalin, as well, and tried to persuade him that 'the technicians, scientific workers, medical men ... aviators, operating engineers, for instance, would and should supply the best material for constructive revolution in the West, and that the dictatorship of the proletariat (as distinct from the dictatorship of technologists) was a residue of old-style thinking – both of which were key themes in *Things to Come*. But Comrade Stalin seemed singularly unimpressed, and in any case *March of Time* wouldn't have had *that* kind of 'world renown' in mind when it referred to 'one of Great Britain's foremost imaginations'.

*England's Hollywood* does, however, provide a fascinating insight into the atmosphere surrounding the making of *Things to Come*. Where the cloth-capped workers were concerned, production stills of the 'attack on the coal and shale pits in the Floss Valley' sequence were circulated with the caption 'Unemployed miners as film actors represent the devastated army after the World War, in *Things to Come*'. Del Strother, who worked as one of the trainee sound engineers on the film, recalled that he was asked to scour the streets of Isleworth to search for undernourished extras to play the victims of 'the wandering sickness' and that he had no problem at all in finding plenty of them: Wells had explicitly requested 'cadaverous people for the sick in the Pestilence Series', and Strother duly obliged. And Korda's new studio at Denham, which promised to manufacture films that would appeal beyond the limited home market, *was* being actively promoted as a major employer and cure for the depression. *The Private Life of Henry VIII* had demonstrated that 'British films with proper British taste [of a sort] and British accents', especially if they were made to look like the American ones by Hungarians with a flair for showmanship, could earn sackfuls of dollars.

Where the studio was concerned, *England's Hollywood* creates the impression that *Things to Come* was a highly appropriate inaugural production at the new facility. In fact, since the sound stages were not completed yet, the huge Everytown Square set was built on the lot at Denham in late spring 1935, and the base of the Space Gun was constructed at the same time on the hill overlooking the lot, but many of the interiors and all the special effects were filmed at Worton Hall Studio in Isleworth, where Korda had specially commissioned a silent stage of 250 × 120 feet (which was moved, intact, to Shepperton Studios in 1948 – where it is still reported to be functioning today). The

The original caption read: 'Unemployed miners as film actors represent the devastated army after the World War'

earliest interiors of *Things to Come* were shot in autumn 1934 at the Consolidated Studio at Elstree (which Korda had hired for the purpose). Other exteriors included a derelict coal-mine in South Wales (the attack on the Hill people) and Brooklands racetrack (the two wrecked planes, following the dogfight between John Cabal's biplane and a single-wing aircraft). But the association between the seven sound stages of Denham Studios, rising out of the rubble of the depressed film industry, and the ultra-modern Everytown rising out of the rubble of world war and the neo-feudal era which succeeds it, was nevertheless a neat one: Bauhaus designer Walter Gropius informally advised Alexander Korda on the layout of the Denham laboratories (the first colour labs in Britain) just as Korda's fellow Hungarian Laszlo Moholy-Nagy had been a consultant to Corvin Studios in the suburbs of Budapest, which Korda had designed and built way back in 1917. And *Things to Come* was certainly the product of 'imagination as well as money': it cost between £250,000 and £300,000 (estimates vary) – by far the most expensive film that Korda, or anyone else in Britain, had produced to date – and it had a shooting schedule of over a year.

As for *March of Time*'s presentation of H. G. Wells, he was

The attack on the coal mine, filmed in South Wales

undoubtedly an 'author of world renown' by the mid-1930s, following a series of pioneering scientific romances, or more precisely scientific speculations couched in the form of best-selling stories, including *The Time Machine* (1895), *The Island of Dr Moreau* (1896), *The Invisible Man* (1897), *The War of the Worlds* (1898), *The First Men in the Moon* (1901), *The Food of the Gods* (1904) and *The War in the Air* (1908), plus a series of polemical exercises in political, scientific and social prediction, or 'imaginative histories', including *Anticipations* (1901), *A Modern Utopia* (1905), *The New Machiavelli* (1911), *The Outline of History* (1920 – which took the story up to the 'aeroplane-radio-linked world' of 1960), *The Science of Life* (1931), *The Work, Wealth and Happiness of Mankind* (1932) and *The Shape of Things to Come* (1933). These had made him an instantly recognisable name among 'a crowd of season-ticket holders … reading Mr Wells' latest in the first class as well as the third class compartment', as T. S. Eliot wrote, with characteristic asperity. The stories sold more, while the prophecies made the headlines. When Wells dropped in on Charlie Chaplin or Stalin or Lenin or whoever happened to be the President of the United States for a well-publicised chat about the meaning of life, it seemed the most natural thing in the world.

But he had *not*, as the newsreel's commentary insisted, 'given up writing books entirely in favour of cinema': it would be impossible to imagine someone as obsessively prolific with the written word even contemplating such a decision. It had recently been said of him that he wrote a new book in the time it took most people to read his last one. Instead, he had turned away from fiction towards the writing of imaginative and provocative histories of the future, based on his own social and scientific background and full of fluent disillusionment with the politics, economics and societies he saw around him: from novelist to prophet. Sometimes his prophecies were open to misinterpretation: those black-shirted aviators looked suspiciously like the followers of Oswald Mosley who goose-stepped along Cable Street in London's East End later that same year. His heroic 'scientific worker' or technocrat in *Things to Come* was even named Oswald – but then again, one of Oswald Cabal's predecessors, the equally visionary Sydenham in the novel *Joan and Peter* (1918), had also been called Oswald. At the same time as extolling the virtues of a black-shirted elite, Wells wrote of the leader of the Bolshevik Revolution in his book *The Shape of Things to Come*: 'One name alone among those who have been prominent in our time escapes to a certain extent the indictment of this history – the name of Nicolai Lenin.' Which must mightily have confused the card-carrying members of the British Union of Fascists.

It was true, as the newsreel commentary said, that Wells had developed a new love affair with the cinema, since Baroness Moura Budberg – his sometime lover and current secretary – had introduced him in 1934 to the notoriously persuasive Alexander Korda over a plate of sardine sandwiches in a Bournemouth teashop, with the result that Wells had signed a contract on a penny-postcard there and then. Other film versions of Wells' stories had been made before this, of course: *The Invisible Thief* (1909) and *First Men in the Moon* (1919), both French; *Kipps* and *The Passionate Friends* (both 1922, and British); *The Island of Lost Souls* (1932) and *The Invisible Man* (1933), made in Hollywood as part of the horror boom of the early sound years. And Wells himself had helped to write three shorts in 1928 – *Bluebottles*, *Daydreams* and *The Tonic* – co-scripted and designed by his son Frank, and which introduced Charles Laughton and Elsa Lanchester to the screen. A year later, he published *The King who was King – the book of the film*, based on a treatment he had written a couple of years before for an abandoned project then called *The Peace of the World*: on the book's jacket he had been quoted as saying, 'I believe that if I had my life over again, I might devote myself entirely to working for the cinema' – which was perhaps where the *March of Time* scriptwriter got the idea from. But Wells categorised the silent film versions of his books as 'amateur efforts'; he had a lot of time for James Whale's *Invisible Man* but this was far from enough to deflect him from a constant stream of literary productions. 'He throws off a history of the world,' wrote Jerome K. Jerome in a famous phrase, 'while the average schoolboy is learning his dates.'

It was often said of Wells that when he fell in love he tended to fall head-over-heels. According to his son Anthony West, he was 'almost sleepless with excitement' at the prospect of turning his weighty non-fiction *Shape of Things to Come* into a story film for Korda called *Whither Mankind?* (the original title) – for that was the project they had mutually agreed in Bournemouth. He started giving interviews to the press, in which he opined that 'the film is likely to oust both the opera and the stage in the long run', and that the development of new techniques of sound and photography would cause 'a very considerable reaction' in the contemporary novel. Cinema, he added – echoing, perhaps unconsciously, the famous words of Lenin – had 'the possibility of becoming the greatest art form that has ever existed'. Its combination of technology and educational potential was irresistible. Korda was delighted. It was all useful publicity and, besides, Wells fascinated him. When the filming of *Things to Come* began in earnest, H. G. was on the set almost every day – and he was usually the first to arrive. Even though he had little or no direct experience of film-making, he had views on everything – script, design, performances, editing and music. And that, once the honeymoon period was over, was to be part of the problem.

For Wells believed fervently in the themes which became embodied in the gigantic treatment of *Whither Mankind?* On 9 January 1934, for example, he had given a BBC broadcast with the similar title *Whither Britain?* in which he had warned listeners of the 'spasm of nationalism which has contracted men's minds' (in the previous two years) and of the dangers of cooping up 'the English mind and English life within the narrow bounds of nationalism. ... We are a world people and we belong to the world.' The long-term solution, he concluded, lay in integrating England in 'one great world unity ... the commonweal of mankind'; also in 'the mighty fabric of modern science which was so largely English in its beginnings', and particularly the aviation industry which '*must be international* ... under a Board of Air Control ... to police the air.' In short, control of world economic reconstruction should be given to 'one great Planning Board'. 'Is that utopian? That is for you to judge. I consider I am talking plainest common sense. And I cannot help reminding you that once or twice in the past I have been a successful prophet.'

For Alexander Korda, the film *Whither Mankind?* may have been a job of work. For H. G. Wells it was an article of faith, as applicable to the rest of the industrialised world as to Britain. The question was whether a prophet of technology could cope with the mechanics and constraints of film-making.

## 2

. . . . . . . . . . . . . . . . . . . . . . . . .

### THINGS AS THEY ARE

H. G. Wells once confided to J. B. Priestley, 'A camel is not a horse designed by a committee; a committee is a camel designed by a horse.' Even though, as one of the great and the good, he had served on many national committees both during and after the First World War, he seemed temperamentally unsuited to any form of collective decision-making which might commit him to not having his own way. He was also famous for being a writer who resented having to revise anything he had produced, even if he had produced it at breakneck speed. Paul Reilly (later to become Director of the Design Council) commissioned some articles from Wells in the mid-1930s, for the *News Chronicle*. He was 'rather difficult to deal with,' Reilly was to recall. 'It wasn't that he was unwilling but that he laid down very strict rules: so much a word, including "a" and "the"; a written agreement not to change anything, not even a comma; and an agreement not to cut anything.' Wells' contract with Alexander Korda for writing the script of *Whither Mankind?* stipulated that not a single word could be altered without the author's express permission, that the author would be guaranteed a say in all aspects of the property's translation to the screen, that he would be credited on the title and paid a royalty for each showing of the film. He was also to be paid £10,000 for the film rights to his original book. Considering that Wells had never previously written a full-length film script, his contract shows just how fascinated with 'H.G.' Korda must have been at the time it was signed.

Raymond Massey, who played the two central roles of the aviator John Cabal and his great-grandson (or grandson – the script, despite numerous revisions, cannot make up its mind), the President of the World Council and Chief Freemason of Science Oswald Cabal, confirmed in his autobiography that:

> Not only had Alex Korda given Wells complete control of the script but he had contractually agreed to his interference in every phase of the production, in the direction, design, cutting, even in the promotion of the finished picture. Wells was not boasting when he referred, as he frequently did, to *my* picture, *my* production and *my* editing; he had the contractual right to do so.

When he would say 'I chose to make this picture', he was just stating a fact. No writer for the screen ever had or ever will have such authority as H. G. Wells possessed in the making of *Things to Come*. Having secured these dictatorial powers, Wells soon found out that he was unable to exercise them. ... He discovered that Korda and his production team were masters in their own departments and needed no help from him.

The resulting tensions, concluded Massey, made this 'the most difficult film I ever worked in' – a perception which was echoed by Korda in a weary aside to John Betjeman, towards the end of the shooting: 'This is the most difficult film to make I've ever come across.'

The characters of John and Oswald Cabal were described in the 'notes for casting' appended to the treatment thus:

John Cabal is a man of 35 with a sensitive, intelligent face and a fine voice, reasonably well built. ... He is the Maker, and the main

H. G. Wells gives advice to the people of the future (Pearl Argyle and Raymond Massey)

figure throughout. He is the Father in the first part, the English aviator in the second part and (as a ripe man of 70) the leader of the revolt in the third part. Oswald Cabal, the principal speaker in the fourth part is his grandson [great-grandson in the text itself]. He is presented by the same actor as John Cabal. He is a man of 38–45, but he is fitter and plainly *healthier* than his grandfather.

When Raymond Massey received this treatment, his first reaction was to be 'appalled' at the scale of his task and at the strangely *abstract* and allusive quality of the writing: 'The picture was fantastically difficult to act,' he wrote, because

> Wells had deliberately formalised the dialogue, particularly in the later sequences. ... Emotion had no place in Wells' new world. I had a marathon acting job. ... We were always the puppets of Wells, completely under his control. ... [In the story] a bad dictatorship would be followed by a benevolent one. A benign big brother was bound to be a bore. He was the fellow I played in the futuristic part of the film. I could only act Oswald Cabal as calmly and quietly as possible ... for six months my skinny legs, bare and knock-kneed, were photographed for posterity on unheated stages and freezing locations.

Vincent Korda's son Michael elaborates:

> Alex did everything he could to please Wells. He agreed to let Wells write the script. He agreed that the movie should be a collaboration. He hired Frank Wells, H. G.'s son [as assistant art director], and he even let Wells do most of the talking at story conferences. As Wells pontificated, in his high, squeaky voice, Alex gradually came to realise that H. G.'s presence might be more of a hindrance than a help, and he was one day heard to remark that 'H. G. is a second Charles Laughton'.... Wells wrote three screen treatments, and many months were spent explaining to him why they could not be made into a film. In the end, Wells had one more try, and Alex surrendered, with significant misgivings. He would make the film as he had promised, exactly as Wells 'dictated'.

Cedric Hardwicke, who in the final section of the film set in the year 2036 played the artist Theotocopulos – distant ancestor, although this esoteric fact was never explained in the final script, of Domenikos Theotocopulos (better known, in Spain, as El Greco) – the incurable romantic who yearns for 'the good old days when life was short and hot and merry, and the devil took the hindmost', remembered in his autobiography *A Victorian in Orbit* a dramatic instance of Wells' 'complete control':

> He had invited me to replace in the picture a distinguished English actor whose performance, already completely filmed, had not been to Wells' liking. The voice of this actor needed more *vox humana*, the author held, and my actor's instinct would not permit me to disagree with him. The one change I suggested was in my costume as Theotocopulos, the reactionary rabble-rouser who tries to destroy the Space Gun.
>
> 'If this is the year 2055 [actually 2036, changed from 2054 in the original treatment],' I argued, 'and cities are filled with skyscrapers and people dress in cloaks and sandals, think how dramatically effective Theotocopulos would be if his hankering for the past made him drive an old Ford car and he dressed like a Wall Street broker? But as I rather anticipated, Wells would not hear of it. Theotocopulos, as played by myself, wore an 'ornate, richly embroidered, coloured satin costume with a great cloak'. That was how the movie 'treatment' described it. My work in *Things to Come* was completed with such speed and lack of ceremony that the actor I had replaced had no idea that his entire performance lay on the cutting-room floor. He arrived with a party of expectant friends at the London premiere [Leicester Square Cinema, 21 February 1936], an exceedingly fashionable gathering. After his disappointment, I remained pleasantly surprised that he did not become my enemy for life.

The actor in question was Ernest Thesiger, fresh from his triumph as the waspish and gay necromancer Dr Praetorius – the one who calmly explained to Karloff's monster that gin was his only weakness – in James Whale's *Bride of Frankenstein* (1935). To judge by surviving production stills of *Things to Come* (which were, it seems, sent out to publicise the film despite the change of casting), the lean-featured Thesiger certainly resembled Wells' description of Theotocopulos as 'a tall, slender man [who] was like one of the figures in a picture by his ancestor El Greco'. But the character of Theotocopulos was also a charismatic crowd-pleaser, a powerful representative of what Wells called 'everydayism', and so Thesiger's reedy, aristocratic voice was not deemed to be suitable. Cedric Hardwicke had the voice, but not the physical appearance, and so in the final version of the film it was his *assistant* who was made up to look like an El Greco figure.

Raymond Massey remembered, rather scurrilously, that in the end Wells realised that the safest thing to do was to restrict his professional participation on the set to 'a close attention to the costumes of the female members of the cast. He would adjust a fold of a skirt or a casual pleat with the touch of a costumier and much more enthusiasm.' In fact, his obsession with detail – even during the later stages of the production – seems to have gone a lot further than that.

Ralph Richardson, who played the Boss – the warlord of Everytown in the guerrilla period following the World War and the

Rival versions of Theotocopulos: Ernest Thesiger (l.) and Cedric Hardwicke (r.)

wandering sickness – had a happier time working with Wells. This was his most substantial film role to date: his debut had been as a jewel thief posing as a jovial vicar in *The Ghoul* (1933), with Cedric Hardwicke *and* Ernest Thesiger, and this had been followed by *The Return of Bulldog Drummond* and *Bulldog Jack* (as a French super-villain in a white wig, who was chased at full speed by Jack Hulbert around the London Underground). Cedric Hardwicke had in fact been instrumental in promoting Richardson to a name above the title, when he recommended this 'exciting young actor' who was also 'a very fast driver of very fast cars' to producer-director Herbert Wilcox eighteen months before he was signed for *Things to Come.*

Richardson was to recall becoming 'very close to Wells. Adored him. ... I remember going to a very smart party and taking a cigarette and dropping it. The hostess swooped over and shrieked "What have you done?" and Wells, of course he was her prize guest, stooped down and picked it up and said, "Madam, *I* dropped it".' The Boss, as described in Wells' treatment, was:

> a heavy, brutish-looking man of the condottiere type. He is in a rough costume between that of a boy scout, a Far West cowboy and a cossack. A rosette is his symbol and it is everywhere present; the last degradation of the English Tudor Rose. He carries himself with a self-conscious swagger. ... The producer should bear in mind that the Boss is *not* intended to be a caricature of a Fascist or Nazi leader. He is as much South American or Haitian or Gold Coast. He is something more ancient, more modern and more universal than any topical movements.

As played by Richardson, the Boss conforms to much of this: brutish, swaggering, bullying, superstitious, posturing and evidently enjoying himself hugely. And much given to saying things like 'We have to stop the pace of the times.' His costume – sheepskin liberty-bodice worn over a second-hand guardsman's tunic (a stage, perhaps, towards the preferred outfit of commandos in the actual Second World War), with a tin hat worn at a jaunty angle – is also in the spirit of Wells, even if it is more cossack than boy scout. But in one important detail Richardson ignored the author's advice. 'I was a picture of Mew-soh-lini,' he remembered. 'Because there *was* no dictator before Mew-soh-lini. He invented the whole thing.' Whether or not Wells was upset by this interpretation, he continued to get on well with the actor. He must have been thrilled that Mussolini himself was so outraged with the characterisation that he personally banned all screenings of the film in Italy. Wells' original book *The Shape of Things to Come* had been rather more friendly towards the Fascist dictatorship: 'At least it insisted upon discipline and public service for its members. It appeared as a counter movement to a chaotic labour communism [with] a considerable boldness in handling education and private property for the public benefit. Fascism indeed was not an altogether bad thing; it was a bad good thing; and Mussolini has left his mark on history.' In the film version, Mew-soh-lini became a bad bad thing, to be contrasted with Oswald Cabal and the freemasons of science, who were a bad good thing or perhaps a good bad thing.

Most of the members of Alexander Korda's team – 'masters in their various departments' or not – were closer to Raymond Massey's experience of Wells than Ralph Richardson's. Indeed, Massey presents the making of the film as a real-life parallel of Wells' story (or was it vice-versa?): a workmanlike, and long-suffering, technical elite takes

The Boss (Ralph Richardson), backed up by his bejewelled mistress Roxana (Margaretta Scott) argues with the Air Dictator (Raymond Massey)

over a confused situation, amid much noise, and makes good professional sense of it. Korda's long-term friend and collaborator, the novelist and playwright Lajos Biró – an ex-diplomat in pre-Communist and Communist Hungary, who had become Korda's most trusted *dramaturg* on all his film projects as well as being the co-writer of *Henry VIII* – was commissioned to turn Wells' huge treatment of *Whither Mankind?* into speakable dialogue and workable stage directions. He wouldn't get any credit for this ('H. G. Wells' *Things to Come*' it had to be), but if Biró was happy about the script, then Korda was happy too. Since Wells himself was later to call Biró 'the scenarist', in his correspondence, we must assume that his prose came back covered in biro, or at least blue pencil, marks.

After reading the original treatment, Biró wrote a long memorandum to his old friend explaining that Wells' words were about abstract ideas rather than characters, that the piece lacked drama, that the characters tended to talk at each other or – as Wells himself put it, at various moments in the treatment – directly 'to the man in the balcony' or 'at the lady in the balcony seats', and that the final section of the story could equally effectively be set in 1934 as 2054. There was a lot of rhetoric, but no detail to build upon. The camera, sound and editing could make up for some of this, he concluded, but it would be dangerous to rely too much on special effects and visuals to carry the audience along. Wells' licence to do as he wished, Biró implied, might well lead Korda to produce a film which was all talk and no emotion or excitement. At that stage in the proceedings, though, Korda was going through his honeymoon period with the great prophet. And in any case he had hired an experienced visualiser, in the shape of the American William Cameron Menzies (son of first generation Scottish immigrants), as director so the problem of turning Wells' prose into a *cinematic* experience had surely been dealt with.

The 38-year-old Menzies was certainly very experienced. He had designed the fantastical Bakst-inspired *The Thief of Bagdad* and *The Taming of the Shrew* for Douglas Fairbanks, *Cobra*, *The Eagle* and *Son of the Sheik* for Rudolph Valentino – among the fifty-eight features on which he had worked as art director since he joined the industry in 1918; he had, as an ex-illustrator of children's books, virtually invented the storyboard; and he had been awarded the first ever Academy Award for 'interior decoration' (as it was then called). His ability to interpret a script in visual terms was legendary in Hollywood: it was said of him that he had been born with a two-inch lens instead of eyes. A chunky, ruddy individual, he was reported to be well organised and easy to get along with on the set. A good team player. 'The whole secret of motion-picture making is in the preparation,' he'd said. 'What comes after that is hard work.' Sometimes he would produce over a thousand thumbnail sketches – or big illustrations for important set-ups – before a foot of film was shot, as if to prove his axiom. The cinematographer James Wong Howe, who had worked with Menzies in 1932, was very struck by his conscientiousness:

> Menzies designed the sets and sketches for the shots; he'd tell you how high the camera should be, he'd even specify the kind of lens he wanted for a particular shot. The set was designed for one specific shot only, if you varied your angle an inch you'd shoot over the top. ... Menzies created the whole look of the film. I simply followed his orders.

It is likely that director of photography Georges Périnal, whom Korda had brought over to England from the Paramount Studio Paris in 1931, had a similar experience. In a lecture on the role of the art director, delivered in the year he won the Oscar and later turned into an article for *Cinematographic Annual*, Menzies had listed what he considered to be the essential qualifications for the job:

> [The art director] must have a knowledge of architecture of all periods and nationalities. He must be able to picturise and make interesting a tenement or a prison. He must be a cartoonist, a costumer, a marine painter, a designer of ships, an interior decorator, a landscape painter, a dramatist, an inventor, an historical, and now, an acoustical expert – in fact, a 'Jack of all trades'.

His own theories, which bound all these skills together, he added, were derived from films where cutting and thoughtful camera angles were emphasised; so the directors who had made the deepest impression on him – for their 'visual power' – were F. W. Murnau (*Faust* and *Sunrise*) and Sergei Eisenstein. He particularly enjoyed low camera angles and extreme close-ups of faces (which had led to a cameraman once saying to him, 'Let's pull back to a long shot and show the chin and hair'). And on one occasion he had fantasised about a film in which the 'setting might even become the hero in the picture, as would be the case, for example, in the filming of such a subject as *The Fall of the House of Usher*'. A film where the designer-director had thought out every visual effect in advance, with the total control of an animator.

Alexander Korda brought Menzies from Hollywood to London precisely *because* of Wells' evident shortcomings as a visualiser. For, as Menzies had written:

> When the art director receives the finished scenario he begins to transpose the written words into a series of mental pictures. As he reads the script he visualises, as nearly as possible, each change of scene, collecting in his mind the opportunities for interesting compositions. He sketches the setting with an eye to the action that will transpire and the emotional effect that is desired. The director, when he places his characters and guides their movements, is composing pictures – still pictures and moving pictures. The costumer, the designer, the set dresser, the decorator, all contribute to the final composition. And last, but not least, the cameraman in the direction of his lighting and the determination of his different points of view, photographs the composition, to which many have contributed. The photoplay as a *pictorial* art is unique ...

In Menzies' scheme of things, then, the author's role ended 'the moment [the director, cameraman and art director] received the script'. Indeed, the best arrangement was for the art director to *contribute* to the story 'as it was being constructed'.

The trouble was that Wells was not aware of his shortcomings. Easygoing Menzies soon discovered that the script's author was 'a very testy man'. He had conferences about the usual continuity sketches (with Vincent Korda and Georges Périnal), but was then showered with drawings by H. G. of where the actors should stand and how they should deport themselves, and memos about how the world of the future must *under no circumstances* look like 'an imaginative utopia, an ideal but impracticable existence'. 'I want,' wrote Wells in February

1935 – not altogether helpfully – 'to convey the effect that the condition of life shown on the screen is a practicable objective; in fact the only sane objective for a reasonable man. Our only hope of achieving a planned world is to get people to realise in the first place that such a thing is possible.' Another memo from Wells to Menzies was rather more lucid: 'This is all wrong. Get it in better perspective. The film is an H. G. WELLS film and your highest best is needed, for the complete realisation of my treatment. Bless you.' On another occasion he wrote that a half-way competent director could supply the 'technical' input which his treatment had – understandably – omitted to include.

Menzies must have felt he was on solid ground where matters of design and composition were concerned. But he was not nearly so confident as a director. Notice how the word 'dramatist' did not feature prominently in his list of an art director's attributes. Fair enough for a well qualified art director, except that his experience as a *director* was much more limited – and Korda had hired him as a director, not as an art director. His experience in this department only went back as far as 1931, when Fox had offered him a contract; since then, he had co-directed six films (the most notable being with Marcel Varnel and Henry King), and temporarily abandoned his career as an art director. These films included the stylish death-ray melodrama *Chandu, the Magician*, starring Bela Lugosi (who had, in spring 1919, briefly served with Alexander Korda and Lajos Bíró on the Communist Directory for the Film Arts in Hungary: Lugosi had then been known as Arisztid Olt, just as Korda was Sándor Laszlo Kellner). So Menzies had never directed a film all by himself. And, even when he'd shared the job with someone else, his heart still seemed to be in art direction. Twentieth Century-Fox designer Lyle Wheeler, who was to work with Menzies in the late 1930s, reckoned that

> generally, art directors don't make good directors.... When Menzies worked as a director, I used to tell him, 'Bill, you're no damn good as a director'. The first thing he would ask for when he came on the set is 'dig me a hole in here', and that's where he would put his camera. He wanted to photograph ceilings and didn't give a damn what the actors were saying.

It is likely, therefore, that Menzies was seriously rattled by Wells' torrent of memos. Even if they did end with the words 'Bless you'. A man who was directing his first solo film – a big one – and who normally enjoyed the give and take of working with fellow professionals on 'the product of a number of minds' had to hold his ground against an irate author who had never written a script before and who had strong views about both direction *and* art direction. A man who wrote ace memos, and who was equally 'testy' (if a little less impressive) face to face. With a contract to back him up. Just how fraught this relationship became is confirmed by notes which Wells wrote in his personal looseleaf diary shortly after the film was released:

> Cameron Menzies was an incompetent director: he loved to get away on location and waste money on irrelevancies; and Korda let this happen. Menzies was a sort of Cecil B. de Mille without his imagination; his mind ran on loud machinery and crowd effects and he had no grasp of my ideas. He was sub-conscious [*sic*] of his own commonness of mind. He avoided every opportunity of talking to me. The most difficult part of this particular film, and the one most stimulating to the imagination, was the phase representing a hundred and twenty years hence [*sic*], but the difficulties of the task of realisation frightened Menzies; he would not get going on that, and he spent most of the available money on an immensely costly elaboration of the earlier two-thirds of the story. He either failed to produce, or he produced so badly that ultimately they had to cut out *a good half of my dramatic scenes*.

This was, of course, unfair. Unless Wells included Denham as a 'location' (since the lengthy task of post-production had taken place at Isleworth), the location work in South Wales and at Brooklands cannot have taken more than a week. The cutting of 'a good half of my dramatic scenes' (see later) was in all probability done because Biró, Korda and most of the actors judged them to be not 'dramatic' enough. The image of Cameron Menzies as a run of DeMille operative obsessed with 'crowd effects' is odd, considering that most of these crowd effects occurred in the last part of the story – the very part which Menzies, apparently, 'failed to produce'. The only comments which ring true are the ones about the director expending much of his visual imagination on 'the earlier two-thirds of the story' – the sequences showing the Christmas Eve bombing of Everytown and the rebuilding of the town are masterpieces of montage, lighting and design – and about Menzies going out of his way to avoid face-to-face confrontations with H. G.

It seems almost incredible that Wells should have been so wide of the mark about the man who would shortly become the first 'production designer' in film history, and who was more responsible for the successful completion of *Gone With the Wind* (over 15 per cent of which he directed, in equally difficult circumstances) than any of the credited directors. On 2 November 1935, a mere five months before he wrote about Menzies in his diary, Wells had been interviewed *in situ* by the American press about his involvement in the film *Things to Come*. The reporters were evidently charmed by his oh-so-British modesty and candour when he kicked things off by stating that he was a mere amateur in the business of film: 'I have only been dealing with the film in the last two years,' he said, 'but I found an opportunity of making a couple of films with Alexander Korda in which I could have a certain voice in the production, and I thought it was worthwhile to come in before it was too late to try my hand at the new art.' At the end of the conversation, Wells was asked whether any alterations had been made to his story and conception of *Things to Come*.

'No,' said Wells.

'Was nothing added or subtracted?'

'No, it was the same as I wrote it.'

And this was at the *end* of the shooting schedule. Perhaps the disparity between Wells' diary and this public statement had something to do with the fact that Wells was contracted by Korda to promote the finished picture. Or perhaps his diary references to Menzies were intended as a defence against the public response to the film; Wells prefaced them by stating that 'it had a considerable success from the commercial point of view', which simply wasn't true. The critics, yes – the public, no. Or perhaps like Charlie Chaplin, who in Wells' view was 'struggling with parallel difficulties to mine', he was quite simply 'a tired man'.

Another member of this ill-matched team, one who – like Biró – was part of the tight-knit clan of Hungarians surrounding the producer, was the 'designer of settings' Vincent Korda. If Alexander Korda sometimes preferred to communicate with Wells in French (interpreted by Baroness Budberg), sometimes in ungrammatical and unpunctuated English, his younger brother never quite managed to master the difference between 'w' and 'v' and so presumably referred throughout the shoot to 'Mr Vells'. The Hungarian director Gabriel Pascal, who was shortly to become as fascinated with George Bernard Shaw as Alexander Korda was with H. G. Wells (occasionally, too, with explosive results), said of Vincent: 'He speaks every language, but badly – except Hungarian, which he speaks terribly.' Vincent Korda would turn up on the set in very expensive suits which looked as shabby and untidy as he could possibly make them – an image which he cultivated to show his executive pin-striped brother that he would just as soon be back in his painting studios in Paris and the south of France – to be greeted by the producer with a friendly 'Re-ally Vincikém'. He would then, according to his son Michael, refer to the carpenters, painters, plasterers and propmen as 'his boys'. The middle brother, Zoltán, was away in Africa directing *Sanders of the River* (1935) for much of this period. Ever since he'd accidentally become separated from his film crew there, he'd become known to initiates as The Lost Korda.

Vincent, who had graduated from Budapest's College of Industrial Art and the city's Academy of Art before studying painting in Vienna and Florence, and – for twelve years – practising as a painter and designer in Paris, had by chance become an art director in 1931 when his brother Alexander asked him to redesign the Marseilles waterfront set for *Marius* in Paris. On that occasion, according to Michael Korda, he'd arrived on the set – hotfoot from Cagnes-sur-Mer – in denims, espadrilles and a straw hat. He had been coaxed to Britain (by Alexander) to head the art department of London Films, and had achieved his first major critical success with his economy sets for *The Private Life of Henry VIII* – which, thanks to his design talent and Georges Périnal's glossy camerawork, had seemed a great deal more expensive than they actually were. According to Edward Carrick (the son of theatre designer Gordon Craig) in *Art and Design in the British Film* (1948), Vincent Korda 'would probably have become a very great painter had he not been engulfed in his brother's work ... and become established as Alexander Korda's Art Director. ... Well known for his generosity, he also helped many young designers to find their way to success [in the film industry].' Carrick added that Vincent tended to be more highly rated among critics than either of his brothers.

R. Myerscough-Walker, in his book *Stage and Film Decor*, written three years after *Things to Come* was released, was less effusive:

> When we discussed recently his views on films, I asked him what led him to change from painting to art direction. His answer, quite simply, was the purely practical reason – money; but, in spite of this misleading remark, there is no question but that he has brought into art direction a quality which is higher in pictorial art than the average designer, in either theatre or films. ... His appearance is conducive to the rumours one hears about the mad antics of the Korda brothers. He looks a man of temperament; and in a film studio he lives up to his appearance, much to the amazement of the English designers. ... The tendency now is, for the most part, to get back to a close co-operation [between director, cameraman and art director] ... In an industry consisting of aggressive males, this is more difficult than it first appears; but Korda is fortunate a) that his name is Korda, and b) that he possesses a personality equal to that of any individual in the film industry. When he works on a film, the director and camera-men are likely, because of this combination, to listen more to his needs than is usual; consequently he is able to achieve some fine results – which you have no doubt seen, in such films as *The Shape of Things to Come*. ... Hence the name that Vincent Korda has in the film industry for being a difficult man.

Vincent Korda himself, in 'The Artist and the Film', an article he wrote for *Sight and Sound* in spring 1934, was eager to dispel this image of the temperamental Hungarian artist who had been let loose on his brother's expensive toy train set, the only one of the Korda brothers who needed to be coaxed into working in the film industry.

> When we talk of 'art' in relation to the film, we must consider it not as a spontaneous and inspired creation, but quite definitely as an 'applied' art, bound in scope by severely practical limitations. ... So soon as an audience exclaims 'what a marvellous set!' the art director has failed in his task. ... Having satisfied the author that the designs for the sets comply with his descriptions; having persuaded the director that they tally with his own conception of

the author's ideas; having proved to the sound engineer that their acoustic properties are satisfactory, and that there will be ample room for his beloved 'mike-boom', there still remains another collaborator to satisfy – namely the camera. And the camera is a hard task-master. Every scene must be designed so that it shall appear to the eye of the camera just as though it were seen through the human eye. ... [The art director] creates the illusion to be registered in the subconscious mind of the audiences, of a world beyond the immediate confines of the set. ... There are a vast number of different aspects of the film art director's job. There are trick effects involving models, back-projection and similar specialised knowledge. But these are incidentals. What really counts is camera consciousness. The artistic value of innumerable productions would be greatly enhanced if more producers would take the art director fully into their confidence in the planning of a film. As it is, too often the poor fellow is expected to achieve miracles overnight.

On *Things to Come*, Vincent Korda certainly enjoyed the confidence of the producer and had a good working relationship with the director of photography. He also, by all accounts, got on well with the craftsmen and technicians at Isleworth and Denham (where the most expensive set, Everytown Square, was built and destroyed). The problem was, of course, 'the author' who needed satisfying that Vincent's visualisations 'complied with his descriptions', and the director who was supposed to have a clear 'conception of the author's ideas'. Actually, the author's *ideas* were crystal clear: it was just that he had provided very few *visual* clues as to how on earth they could be realised.

For the final section of the treatment, 'The World in 2054', Wells kept referring to 'fresh spectacular effects' and reiterating that 'if they are not surprising and magnificent and REAL, the whole film falls down', or 'the scene must be sensationally better and *different* from any contemporary scene or the film will fall down', or 'here the aeroplane designer gets his chance', or 'this is the dress designer's best chance, so let it be taken'. And so on. The result, according to Michael Korda, was that while Vincent worked long and hard at turning the treatment of *Whither Mankind?* into workable 'screen effects', Wells seemed to be carrying a generalised 'vision of the future' in his head which proved extremely difficult to turn into practical reality. In consequence, the author kept on making 'minute changes, for he was determined that the movie should represent his vision of the future accurately. ... He fussed over the costumes, and worried about whether the aeroplanes of the future would have propellers or not. Vincent endured all this stoically.' Which did not come naturally to him. Perhaps he realised, after reading the treatment, that there was absolutely no point in carrying on like El Greco if he wanted to get anywhere with the prophet of the coming scientific age. Wells was a writer who had a justifiable reputation for communicating big ideas in clear, no-nonsense prose; on this occasion, however, he seemed to have both his feet planted firmly in the air. He had plenty of *ideas*, but lacked the experience of knowing how they could be 'registered in the subconscious mind of the audience'.

Some of these ideas concerned the music for the film, and in this department Wells was particularly keen to find ways of getting to the emotions of the people in the stalls *and* the balcony. On the very first page of his original treatment he described the story in musical terms, and made it clear that the structure of *Whither Mankind?* should resemble a cinematic and dramatic opera, with the long speeches functioning as recitatives and the great set-pieces having entirely orchestral accompaniments. The four main parts of the film – 'roughly following the anticipations in *The Shape of Things to Come*' – should, he wrote, appear as follows:

The first part (*Pastorale*) represents *A Christmas Party* under (practically) PRESENT CONDITIONS. No date. War breaks out and the chief character reappears in the second part (*Marche Funèbre*). The Episode of the Two Aviators (1940). A series of short exposures then shows war, degenerating into SOCIAL CHAOS, leading to the third part, which begins in *The Darkest Hour of the Pestilence*, shows *The Wandering Sickness at its Climax* (1960), and the revolt of the air-men, technicians and men of science, who achieve *Reconstruction amidst the Ruins* (1970). This third part is set in A SPECTACLE OF IMMENSE RUIN. Everything is done to summon up a vision of our present world *smashed*. Then comes a rapid series to convey WORK, leading up to the counter vision of what can be done with our world. ... The fourth part (*Chorale*) is THE WORLD IN 2054. This concentrates on fresh spectacular effects. ... The interest of this latter part brings the drama of creative effort versus the resistances of jealousy, indolence and sentimentality, to a culmination. This fourth part must carry an effective answer to the question 'And after all, when you have unified the world, is it going to be any different from what it is today?' The answer is Yes. The spirit will be different.

The false sense of security of the present day was, in musical terms, a *Pastorale* at Christmas time. This would be rudely interrupted by war and disintegration: a *Marche Funèbre*. Then the reconstruction of the world in the musical form of 'a rapid series', consisting of 'hammerings and molten metal, etc.', leading to the construction of great buildings and engineering works. Finally, a hymn of praise to the benefits of progress – through the impact of science and technology ('creative effort') – a hundred and twenty years hence, or thereabouts: a magnificent *Chorale*. It was important, wrote Wells, for sound sequences and picture sequences to be 'closely interwoven' to achieve these effects. So the music should not be 'tacked on; it is part of the design'.

H. G. Wells had met Arthur Bliss in March 1934, at the Royal Institution in London, where Bliss was giving a lecture, one of a series, on 'Aspects of Contemporary Music'. The audience, the lecturer recalled, was 'bristling with ear trumpets and bath chairs ... a fearsome-looking audience', and the theme of the series was that 'the foundation of all music is emotion, and that without the capacity for deep and subtle emotion a composer only employs half the resources of his medium.' Some modern composers were happy just to please themselves, he said, but he was convinced that direct

Composer Arthur Bliss (l.) discusses the score with arranger Muir Mathieson

communication with listeners, at the emotional rather than the intellectual level, was the main challenge of contemporary composition. He was lecturing as a well-known progressive musician (influenced by modern jazz) who was about to enter the establishment phase of his career, with a Professorship, the Directorship of Music at the BBC in wartime, and ultimately the Mastership of the Queen's Musick in 1953. Whether this particular lecture struck a chord with Wells as a popular and accessible writer on advanced themes Bliss, wasn't sure. In his autobiography, *As I Remember*, he wrote:

> I do not know why [Wells] honoured the occasion, as admittedly music meant little to him; perhaps he came to see how another speaker endured the ordeal of this special audience, for later when I knew him he confessed that from sheer nervousness he himself had dried up after twenty-five minutes, and had had abruptly to leave the lecture hall. Something that I said on this occasion must have caught Wells' attention, for he invited me to lunch, and there and then spoke of his projected film based on his book *The Shape of Things to Come*, and asked me whether I would like to collaborate with him by writing the musical score.

This was an imaginative suggestion, because Bliss had never written 'music for the films' before. But as Wells knew, a similar arrangement on a smaller scale had worked well when John Grierson had approached Benjamin Britten to score some of his GPO documentaries. By 13 April, Wells was already expressing delight, in a letter, that Arthur Bliss was 'biting on the Film': 'I'm being very driven just now by details, but a little later I shall be only too keen to come and hear some of the work you have done. God bless our efforts – H. G.'

Two months later, following a piano recital of work-in-progress at Bliss's home in Hampstead, Wells wrote again – a little more formally – after 'digesting my impressions':

> Of all the early part up to and including the establishment of the Air Dictatorship I continue to be confident and delighted. But I am not so sure of the Finale. Perhaps I dream of something superhuman but I do not feel that what you have done so far fully renders all that you can do in the way of human exaltation. It's

good – nothing you do can fail to be good – but it is not yet that exultant shout of human resolution that might be there – not the marching song of a new world of conquest among the atoms and stars. I know that if you say 'This is only provisional' presently something will come – between sleeping and waking, or when you are walking in the country, or in a railway train – or shaving – which will be the crowning air of *Whither Mankind?* Biró I think is very much of my mind on this. Trumpets!

Yours ever, H. G. Wells.

Bliss evidently took the criticism well. He was later to recall that 'although [Wells] knew next to nothing about musical technique, he had a genius for putting his finger on a weak spot, for pointing out a slack thought. I treasure letters and postcards from him during that time, written in his small and squiggly hand, and containing a mass of directions and hints, some of which, I fear, were frankly impractical.' Perhaps the exultant shout of human resolution which was to conclude the film was one of them. It was the same problem which the director, the designer and the *dramaturg* were all simultaneously encountering in their dealings with H. G.: how to put over Wells' 'new world of conquest among the atoms and stars' in ways which would match the author's high and highly unfocused expectations. Evidently Bliss wrote to say he would do his best, for on 5 July, Wells wrote him a more relaxed note saying, 'I'm so glad you agree. I'm sure the great thing will come all right. Bless you, H. G.'

But Wells wasn't the only one who knew next to nothing about music. Alexander Korda appears to have had an entirely pragmatic approach to the relationship between music and image and so had great difficulty in comprehending the idea (now shared by both Wells and Bliss) that the score was 'part of the design'. The composer recalled, in an interview in 1974:

Alexander Korda wasn't musical in any sense. When you, for instance, saw a posse of police on motor bikes rushing up the road [in the Christmas Eve sequence] he felt that you must have the exact sound of these. I said, 'Alex, by all means!' 'Yes,' he said, 'but I want the music too.' And I said, 'You know, you can't have it – you will either have the bikes and hear the exhausts or else I'll try to do it in music.' But he insisted, 'I must have both', and of course I had to give way. That's the kind of thing which is to the composer ... frustrating. You think – what's the use?

By October 1934 these two opposing philosophies of film music had come out into the open. Wells was keen to record the music score in advance – and construct the film around it – while Korda preferred to leave the score in its present provisional state and recall the composer at the post-production stage. The letter which brought Bliss up to date on the negotiations with London Films is worth quoting in full (Bliss, in his autobiography, only published part of it):

October 17th, 1934

Dear Bliss

You have heard little or nothing from London Films for some time. Much has been doing in the way of preparatory work and production will certainly begin before December. We are taking the Alexandra Palace for some of the long shots [in fact Everytown was built at Denham, and the city of the future was created with miniatures at Isleworth].

*Now* between ourselves.

I am at issue with Korda and one or two others of the group on the question of where and when you come in. They say – it is the Hollywood tradition – 'We make the film right up to cutting. Then *when* we have cut, the musician comes in and *puts on his music.*'

I say 'Balls!' (I have the enthusiastic support of Grierson who makes Post Office films in *that*). I say 'A Film is a composition and the musical composer is an integral part of the design. I want Bliss to be in touch throughout.' I don't think Korda has much of an ear but I want the audience at the end not to know what it sees from what it hears. I want to end on a complete sensuous and emotional synthesis.

Consequently I am sending you Treatment (Second Version). It is very different from the first and in particular the crescendo up to the firing of the *Space Gun* (q.v.) is newly conceived. I think we ought to have a Prelude going on to the end of Reel 1 – But I won't invade your province.

Will you read this new Treatment and then have a talk with me sometime next week. Then when we two have got together a bit we will bring in Biró the Scenarist and then Menzies and my son who are busy on the scenes and have already a definite series of drawings and models [no mention of Vincent Korda]. You will then get the confluent effect systems of

1. Christmas Jollity
2. Onset of the War. WAR.
3. Ruin.
4. Pestilence.
5. Post pestilence *Squalor*.
6. Entry of the Airmen. Struggle of the Airmen.
   Triumph of the new Order.
7. The New World.
   Crescendo of conflict up to the Space Gun.

So far from regarding the music as trimming to be put on afterwards I am eager to get any suggestions I can from you as to the main design. You will see there is now a much more definite conflict in the last part – a sort of Chopinesque *Revolutionary Etude* protest against the simple grand intention of the Space Gun [this is a reference to the revolutionary anthem – 'either the Marseillaise or something like that' – which the followers of Theotocopulos, who are 'not proletarians, but ... rather on the artistic side', were to sing as they marched towards the Gun – subsequently dropped].

Yours ever,
H. G.

In the event, the five and a half-minute dialogue-free sequence showing the rebuilding of Everytown – the 'rapid series to convey WORK' *was* shot and edited to Bliss's musical score. It begins with giant machines tearing out an underground site, then, after various transformation effects, shows more advanced machines effortlessly constructing the city of the future out of prefabricated parts; the score, meanwhile, begins with hammerings and repetitive musical phrases and moves on to the more restful, unhurried rhythms of the future, culminating in a triumphant fanfare. The other great music-and-image sequence is the opening, Eisenstein-inspired montage, which contrasts the jollity of Christmas Eve ('The First Noel', 'God Rest You Merry Gentlemen', 'While Shepherds Watched Their Flocks', plus images of a small boy looking in a shop window, a holly vendor, a butcher selling turkeys) with the sinister rumours of war which are in the air (military drum and trumpet sounds, as newspaper posters announce 'Europe is Arming', 'War scare – latest news', and '10,000 fighters'). This could not have been based on the score Bliss wrote in 1934, however, since the sequence did not appear as such in Wells' treatment. It first appeared in the shooting script in early 1935, and was filmed with the composer's earlier musical ideas in mind.

The outline work which Bliss had completed by autumn 1934 – 'the dramatic *Stimmung* of each section', as contained more or less in Wells' original treatment – remained largely unaltered. But as Bliss recalled, 'many later modifications had, of course, to be made' in post-production. These were mostly organised by the young Scots conductor Muir Mathieson, in a cottage on the building site of Denham Studios, and recorded by the London Symphony Orchestra (under Mathieson's direction) at Denham when the first sound studios were ready. 'It is a fatiguing and anxious job fitting music to a film,' continued Bliss in his autobiography, 'and I used greatly to admire Muir at work, baton in one hand, stop watch in the other, one eye on the film and the other on his players.'

So Wells could say 'Balls!' to his heart's content, but 'the Hollywood tradition' won the day. And even where he *did* win his point, he was by no means convinced that the resulting sequence matched his stratospheric expectations of either the composer or the visualisers, as Bliss was to remember:

> The scene showed the earth being mined, roads made, houses erected, apparently without the aid of manual labour. This was one of the parts of the film in which Wells took a particular interest, watching the 'rushes' as they were shown, and caustically commenting. He had expressed a wish to hear my music before the 'shooting', so I invited him to come to my house in Hampstead, and there played the music through to him as best I could on the piano. I think at the end his comment was, without doubt, the strangest I have ever heard from any critical listener.

'Bliss,' he said, 'I am sure that all this is very fine music, but I'm afraid you have missed the whole point. You see, the machines of the future will be *noiseless!*' Assuring him that I would try to write music that expressed inaudibility I went my own way, and luckily Wells forgot his objections.

It was strange that Wells should have wanted the machines to be silent, since he wanted the rest of the film to be so very talkative. But as a prophet he was, of course, right: digital/electronic technology *does* make less noise than steam-powered technology. As for the final *Chorale*, Wells' comments have not been recorded. The 'exultant shout of human resolution' was to turn into a full-blown chorus of the words 'Which Shall It Be?' repeated over shots of a starry sky.

In retrospect, Arthur Bliss was to describe the experience of working on *Things to Come* as 'six months of adventure':

> To begin with, it was an adventure to see Wells himself at work. He was a man of tireless curiosity. For him, and for me, it was a plunge into a new world, and he was always interested in the new. He was constantly in the studios, suggesting, criticising, stimulating all and sundry.

This reminiscence comes from the composer's introductory talk to a BBC Radio concert broadcast on 15 November 1950, for by then the suite of music from *Things to Come* had become a standard part of his repertoire. It had been issued on records at the time of the film's first release (the first British soundtrack album, and one of the first, for a non-musical, in the world – 'separately performed for gramophone') and Bliss's correspondence shows that selections from the music proved very popular with concert audiences in wartime, during the composer's Directorship at the BBC: 'To Scotland again for *Things to Come*'; 'Conducted the Hallé in *Things to Come*'; 'Conduct the Military Band in a programme of *Things to Come*.' It is ironic that the *March* from the film should have become an evergreen for military bands at this time, for it was originally written to accompany the 'barbaric' flag-waving of the neo-fascist Boss after his hollow victory against the Hill People. In his introductory talk, Bliss described his concert version:

> I have chosen six selections. ... The first accompanies the

Christmas scene at the outset. Young children are playing round a Christmas tree, while their elders are examining with amusement some of the toys, among them models of tanks and aeroplanes. This leads them to discuss whether war were possible with such destructive weapons. I call this first piece *Ballet for Children*. This Christmas scene is interrupted by the sudden air attack. The scene changes to a crowded street in the theatre district (it might be Piccadilly Circus or Broadway), and the film, accompanied by realistic sound as well as by the music [including that posse of police motorbikes] shows bombs falling and buildings crashing (*The Attack*). Wells wished to show that, whether victors or vanquished, all suffer equally from the destruction of scientific knowledge and the break-up of medical safeguards. The long years of war bring a pestilence (*The Pestilence*). The remaining three pieces in this suite deal with the new world as seen through Wells' imagination. The first attempts to regain order and sanity are accompanied by the following *Theme of Reconstruction*. Gigantic machines rebuild the world anew. We see hills levelled, the earth mined, houses built, power supplied, all apparently without the visible control of human beings. Wells was particularly keen to secure the appropriate music for this sequence ... of almost-human monsters (*The Machines*). The final movement is a *March*, which served as a motto theme for the whole film.

Two important selections were not included, presumably because they depended too much on the visual images which had accompanied them: the opening Christmas Eve montage (which preceded the children's party) and the final *Chorale*. In order to make sense of the latter, Bliss would have had to bring Raymond Massey (as Oswald Cabal) and Edward Chapman (as Raymond Passworthy) into the BBC studio, to act out the terrible beauty of the words:

PASSWORTHY: But – we're such little creatures. Poor humanity, so fragile, so weak – little, little *animals*.
CABAL: Little animals – And if we're no more than animals we must snatch each little scrap of happiness and live and suffer and pass, mattering no more than all the other animals do or have

done. (He looks down) It is this or that. (He looks up to the skies). All the Universe is nothingness.

|                   | Which shall it be, Passworthy? |
|                   | Which shall it be? |
| (Musical chorus)  | WHICH SHALL IT BE? |
|                   | WHICH SHALL IT BE? |
|                   | WHICH SHALL IT BE? |

Trumpets, over a shot of 'the starry sky'.

Whether H. G. Wells was, in the end, happy with this 'exultant shout of human resolution', Arthur Bliss never recalled. But at least he got his trumpets.

# 3
........................
## THINGS TO COME

One of the many testy memoranda circulated by H. G. Wells before and during production to 'everyone concerned in designing and making the costumes, decoration, etc. for the concluding phase of *Things to Come*' concerned the basic principles which were to be observed by all those members of Korda's team who were responsible for making visible Wells' prophetic ideas and which 'as yet do not seem to be as clearly grasped as they must be':

I make no apology therefore for reiterating these principles now as emphatically as possible. The first is this, that in the final scenes we are presenting a higher phase of civilisation than the present, where there is greater wealth, finer order, higher efficiency. Human affairs in that more organised world will not be hurried, they will not be crowded, there will be more leisure, more dignity. The rush and jumble and strain of contemporary life due to the uncontrolled effects of mechanism, are not to be raised to the $n$th power. On the contrary they are to be eliminated. Things, structures in general, will be great, yes, but they will not be monstrous. ... All the balderdash one finds in such a film as Fritz Lange's [*sic*] *Metropolis* about 'robot workers'

*Overleaf:* 'Which shall it be, Passworthy? Which shall it be?'

4 5

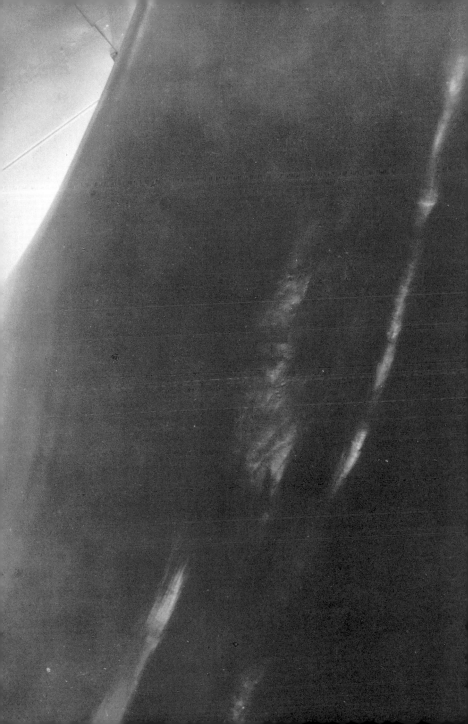

and ultra skyscrapers etc. etc. should be cleared out of your minds before you work on this film. As a general rule you may take it that whatever Lange did in *Metropolis* is the exact contrary of what we want done here. ... 'Common people' generally in the past were infinitely more uniform and 'mechanical' than any people in the future will be. Machinery has superseded the subjugation and 'mechanisation' of human beings. *Please keep that in mind.* The workers to be shown are individualised workers doing responsible co-operative team work. And *work will be unobtrusive* in the coming civilisation. ... There we have the guiding rules to observe . . . but within these limitations and style I would say to *our designers*: 'For God's sake let yourselves go'.

This memorandum – which Wells subsequently issued to the *New York Times* for publication on 12 April 1936, and which he appended to his book version of *Things to Come – a film story* (late 1935) – makes clear what he *didn't* want to see on the screen. He didn't want zombie-like ranks of operatives shuffling to work in shifts of ten hours; he didn't want the hustle and chaos of contemporary New York writ large; he

A vision of New York – 'all sticking up and full of windows' – *not* what Wells wanted as the vision of the future

didn't want buildings which went upwards and a city sectored into workers' dwellings and Roman-style catacombs (down below), the consumer base (street level), and pleasure gardens for the bosses (up above); he didn't want housing for the poor and houses for the rich; he didn't want the vertical social stratification of today projected into the future; and he didn't want a trite moral message – which he considered 'intellectually lazy' – about how if only the head, the heart and the hand could learn to get on better, things would improve. His hero wasn't to be *all heart* – like the young man in jodhpurs who rushes around the machine-room like a mad thing in *Metropolis*. His hero was to be a clear-headed *scientist* who had digested the literature on *industrial efficiency*. In short, his version of the future was to be a utopia not a dystopia: Fritz Lang's version, Wells thought, was based on a tourist viewing of the Manhattan skyline (interestingly, the *New York Times* cut out the line about 'the balderdash ... about ultra skyscrapers, etc. etc.', but kept the misspelling of Lang) and so had not succeeded in seeing beyond things as they are. It was a dystopia with a happy ending tacked onto the end, interspersed with ill-digested references to the Bible.

When H. G. Wells first saw *Metropolis* in April 1927, the film had made him furious – not just because the film-makers hadn't done any social research, but because instead they appeared to have gleaned their ideas about 'air and happiness above, servile toilers below' from his own book of 1899, *When the Sleeper Awakes*, which he now disowned:

> I have recently seen the silliest film. I do not believe it would be possible to make one sillier. ... It gives in one eddying concentration almost every possible foolishness, *cliché*, platitude, and muddlement about mechanical progress and progress in general served up with a sauce of sentimentality that is all its own. ... Possibly I dislike this soupy whirlpool none the less because I find decaying fragments of my own juvenile work of thirty years ago, *The Sleeper Awakes*, floating about in it. Karel Capek's Robots [from the play *R.U.R.* or *Rossum's Universal Robots*, which in 1922 had introduced the word *robot* – from *robotit*: to drudge – into the language] have been lifted without apology, and that soulless mechanical monster of Mary Shelley's, who has fathered so many German inventions, breeds once more in this confusion. Originality there is none. Independent thought, none.

Where nobody has imagined for them, the authors have simply fallen back on contemporary things. The aeroplanes that wander about above the great city show no advance on contemporary types, though all that stuff could have been livened up immensely with a few helicopters and vertical and unexpected movements. The motorcars are 1926 models or earlier. ... After the worst traditions of the cinema world, monstrously self-satisfied and self-sufficient, convinced of the power of loud advertisement to put things over with the public, and with no fear of searching criticism in their minds, [the film people at Ufa] set to work in their huge studio to produce furlong after furlong of this ignorant, old-fashioned balderdash, and ruin the market for any better film along these lines. ... The waste of it!

This review – which stimulated lively responses from various fellow members of the Film Society (a pioneering Society based in London of which Wells, perhaps surprisingly, was a founder member) – became incorporated in Wells' *The Way the World is Going* (1929), which was in part a reply to *Metropolis*. Wells omitted to point out in it that the idea of underground machine-rooms servicing – and subtly enslaving – an above-ground élite had probably originated in another, better-known 'juvenile work' of thirty years before, namely *The Time Machine*. But the review, like his memo to the design team on *Things to Come*, is interesting for the way it reiterates Wells' obsession with the thought that the future *must not seem contemporary* – with ultra skyscrapers, current labour disputes, the trauma of de-skilling, and so on: the future will not involve the contemporary world dressed up in futuristic sets; it will be *structured* differently. In his dealings with Alexander Korda's team, he was generally better at saying what he *didn't* want than at clarifying what he *did*.

He didn't like Aldous Huxley's *Brave New World* (1932), for example, and made clear in the treatment that the artist figure Theotocopulos was intended to represent the high-table intellectualism and 'alarmist fantasies' of Huxley's reaction to the new technologies. *Brave New World* was also explicitly associated with old-style, 'romantic' attitudes to the women of the future – in a discussion of 'the love interest' and patriarchy which was unfortunately cut from the final print of the film:

ROXANA: You want an *impossible* world. ... You are asking too
much of men and women. ... I know men. Every man wants the
same thing – glory! Glory in some form. The glory of being
loved – don't I know it? The glory they love most of all. The
glory of bossing things here – the glory of war and victory. This
brave new world of yours will never come. ... Why should we
work and toil for men? Let them work and toil for us.
MARY HARDING: But we can work *with* them!

The book, *The Shape of Things to Come*, despite its title, had not
contained many visual clues as to how this world of the future might
look and what the things of the future might be. It was an imaginative
history of the next century, subtitled *An Outline of the Future*, in the form
of a dream manuscript left behind in 1930 by Dr Philip Raven, a Balliol
scholar (like Aldous Huxley) and diplomat with the League of Nations.
Raven's dream appears to describe events which take place between the
years 1930 and 2106. In the manuscript, wrote Wells, 'there is much
more attention given to operating forces and much less to mere events
than would be the case in a contemporary student's history. ... There
are studies of typical personalities, but it is relatively very free from
anecdotalism. It is much more scientific.' And so, although there are a
few lapses into 'anecdotalism' – such as the dropping of the gas of peace
onto Pope Alban III, as he blesses three new aeroplanes in Ostia, by an
over-zealous member of the new air police – the book is really about
long-term trends and the political/economic forces which propel them.
The few visual clues there are, tend to be expressed as concepts rather
than as plastic form.

In *Book the First – Today and Tomorrow: the age of frustration dawns*,
which deals with the decline of European civilisation amid the in-
fighting of 'sixty-odd sovereign governments', the prevailing
architectural style is described as one gigantic air-raid shelter:

The world, which had been far too stupid to realize in 1930 that
the direct way out of its economic difficulties lay in the
modernization and rebuilding of its houses, set itself, in a state of
war panic after 1942, to as complete a revision of its architecture
in the face of bombs and gas as its deepening impoverishment
permitted. What it would not do for prosperity, it attempted

belatedly out of fear. The most obvious undertaking was the construction of immense usually ill-built concrete cavern systems for refuge. ... So strong were the influences of that time that even up to 2020 the tendency of architectural design was to crouch. That period has been called, not unjustly, Second Egyptian.

*Book the Second – The Days after Tomorrow: the age of frustration* concerns the outbreak of the Second World War in 1940 – the result of economic nationalism, rearmament with the latest weapons (especially gas bombs), increasing intolerance, casino capitalism and the failure of global talks – and its rapid spread across Europe and the Japanese sector, followed nine years later by a world epidemic of 'the wandering sickness' and the rise of petty warlord states run by gangster-politicians:

First one thing went and then another . . . and the mass of Europeans were even more congested and dirty in their domestic accommodation than they had been before the conflict. ... [On market day in Lyons in 1959], a bearded man leads a couple of

The horse-drawn Rolls Royce

oxen harnessed to a small 'runabout' car in which a corpulent woman sits in front with a crate of ducklings while behind is a netted calf.

This image found its way into the film (where it became a horse-drawn Rolls Royce), as did the image dating from the same historical period of 'the beautiful St Paul's Cathedral ... collapsed in ruin and perished in flame'.

*Book the Third  The World Renascence: the birth of the modern state* is about the ideas and strategies of the union of 'technical revolutionaries' who seize control of the air routes across the world as a prelude to rebuilding the New World Order. They are the 'samurai' of the 1960s and 1970s, and they organise themselves into a Council for World Affairs at two historic conferences held at Basra in Iraq. In this *Book*, Wells combined two of his great passions: aeroplanes and their pilots as key images of modernity, and the role of Iraqi scientists and philosophers in medieval times – when Europe was still struggling out of the dark ages. The 'technical revolutionaries' – who are described as resembling the medieval masons who made the Gothic cathedrals, only with 'a sense of politics' this time round – have suitably ambitious plans for the environment. There will be:

> ... a steady rise in the standard of living and particularly ... 'the rebuilding of the world', new cities, new roads, continually renewed houses everywhere. This was foreshadowed to a certain extent by the German housing schemes in operation as early as the late Twenties, schemes ultimately strangled by the budget-balancing fanatics.

In *Book the Fourth – the Modern State Militant*, pieced together from Dr Raven's 'untidy mass of notes' which 'came through his mind with difficulty, and against resistances', the Second World Council crushes all opposition – through a mixture of armed force, political executions (47,000 in twenty-nine years), the persecution of religious and nationalist minorities, eugenics and 'mental disinfection' or state propaganda. The Council comes to be known, as a result, as the 'Air Dictatorship'. The artist/designer Ariston Theotocopulos, in his private notebooks, argues forcefully that the regime has ignored the aesthetic dimension of life and lost all 'sense of proportion'. Wells clearly has a lot of sympathy with him. The 'Air Dictatorship' may be necessary, as an alternative to 'chaotic barbarism and final extinction', but its human cost is far too high. Dr Raven, who is Jewish, appears to have agreed.

The Council approaches the question of urban planning with fanatical idealism and ever more powerful bulldozers:

> These scientific Puritans produced some of the clumsiest architecture, the most gaunt and ungainly housing blocks, the dullest forests, endless vistas of straight stems, and the vastest, most hideous dams and power-stations, pylon-lines, pipe-lines and so forth that the planet has ever borne.

*Book the Fifth – the Modern State in control of life*, the shortest section of *The Shape of Things to Come*, describes how the planet becomes one world in the post-Dictatorship era from 2059 to 2106: 'racial prejudice is replaced by racial understanding', Basic English becomes the universal language, religions are 'watered down to modernity', genetic engineering produces new foodstuffs and plants (and is forbidden to be used on human beings), a new system of distribution is introduced – based on the model of the department store – and the 'Science of Significs' as applied to linguistics, together with Social Psychology, become the organising intellectual systems. In this period of world government, writes Wells, 'Leonardo da Vinci with his immense

5 4    Costume design (l.) for the Air Dictator, as he arrives in Everytown in his World Transport plane

breadth of vision, his creative fervour, his curiosity, his power of intensive work, was the precursor of the ordinary man as the world is now producing him.'

> Industrial enterprises that formerly befouled the world with smoke, refuse and cinderheaps, are now cleaner in their habits than a well-trained cat. ... The towns grow larger, finer and more varied. ... The last of the ancient skyscrapers, the Empire State Building, is even now under demolition in 2106. ... clearing away is the primary characteristic of the Modern Age.

In adapting this huge book of 'revolution and world government' (as he put it) into a film treatment, Wells decided in the end to concentrate on three main historical periods, and to compress the time-scale: the outbreak of the Second World War, the bandit era and arrival of the airmen, and the city in 2036. The treatment had originally divided the 'Everytown of the future' sequences into two distinct halves – one at the end of the Air Dictatorship, the other in 2054 when 'the creative forces in mankind have triumphed and the face of the earth has changed', a time of 'serenity and beauty' rather than rebuilding. But in the shooting script these two halves turned into the wordless 'Work' interlude followed immediately by Everytown in 2036 – which created problems because it meant that the Air Dictatorship, the world renascence *and* the post-modern era had to take place at much the same time in film terms (which certainly confused the critics, because it gave the impression that Wells was wholeheartedly *in favour of* the Dictatorship, that Oswald Cabal was still using dictatorial methods, and that Theotocopulos's criticisms were entirely out of order – none of which was true to the book).

He also turned some of the great debates of *The Shape of Things to Come* into symbolic characters: Cabal the Maker and Organiser, Passworthy the Time-Server, Roxana the Romantic, Harding the Researcher, Gordon the Mechanic and so on. His original idea had been to hold the story together by following the fortunes of *three* such characters, treated equally – the Maker, the Time-Server and the Researcher – but this was whittled down to one main character (Cabal) with occasional reference to the others who simply gave Cabal the opportunity to show how superior he was. Wells gave extra drama to the 'Space Gun' debate, by making Cabal's daughter and Passworthy's son the first astronauts – an idea he may have derived from the last reel of Maurice Elvey's *The Tunnel* (which was released while he was tinkering with his treatment), where the Engineer (Richard Dix) sacrifices his son on a similarly visionary project.

In this adaptation process, the prophet chose to jettison some of his more radical themes – the critique of competitive capitalism and liberal democracy, the attack on organised religion, the destruction of nationalism – and all his discussions of revolutionary strategy and tactics. He retained and even expanded the debate about gender roles in the future world, as we have seen, but this was cut out of the finished film for reasons of length – thus creating the impression, in science fiction writer Frederik Pohl's words, that 'all the women [of 2036] who had any perceptible work at all were helpers of men; the rest were conspicuously unemployed. Oddly [given Wells' preferences] they were also quite sexless. If they toiled not, neither did they sin.'

The treatment, like the book, mainly consists of broad-brush speculations about the future – albeit expressed in dialogue form – with a few asides to 'the producers' about how best to visualise them. Again, these asides tend to be about concepts and atmospheres, although occasionally they focus on one particular detail; it would take a lot of imagination to turn them into a workable design brief. In the sections dealing with the distant future, which Wells had clearly thought most about, the treatment waxes lyrical about the technology of things to come and the 'general impression' it was intended to create.

*Credit titles*: There shouldn't be any, because 'few people remember the names that are just flashed on the screen'; instead members of the audience should be issued with a programme – including a Wellsian manifesto about the purposes of the film. Only the title, including the name 'H. G. Wells', should appear.

*Market Square of Everytown* ('vaguely about 1940'): 'modern types of facades, but possibly novel advertisements with novel words, e.g. Colour Cinema, Cinema Opera, Wright's Neuro Laxative . . .'

*John Cabal's study*: 'Diagrams and models indicate an engineer. The blade of a propellor over the mantel and other objects emphasise his association with the airforce.'

*War*: '. . . glimpse of the little boy multiplies itself and carries on to an effect of marching armies – battleships, giant caterpillar guns, tanks meet gas, squadron after squadron of warplanes.'

*Gas is Overhead*: 'Horror of the gas made plain. Chaos in the street like the description of Unter den Linden in the *Shape of Things to Come*.' This description, which purports in the book to have been written by the novelist Sinclair Lewis (1885–1990; in fact he died in 1951) shows how the peaceful inhabitants of Berlin meet their deaths in the Second World War: it is terrifyingly ironic, in the light of future events in Germany.

> We went down Unter den Linden and along the Sieges Allee, and the bodies of people were lying everywhere, men, women and children, not scattered evenly, but bunched together very curiously in heaps, as though their last effort had been to climb on to each other for help. This attempt to get close to someone seems to be characteristic of death by this particular gas. Something must happen in the mind. Everyone was crumpled up in the same fashion and nearly all had vomited blood. The stench was dreadful . . .

(In the film, the 'horror of the gas' would be toned down into the less graphic horror of conventional aerial bombing, although, as many critics pointed out, it still remained very frightening.)

*Social Disorder*: 'The idea is now to present our contemporary world *wrecked*. . . . Flashes of ruined capital cities. Possibly of well-known places and structures, e.g. the Eiffel Tower prostrate. The Tower of London destroyed. Brooklyn Bridge down.'
(In the film the main square of Everytown is supposed to stand in for *any* capital city – even though it resembles Piccadilly Circus with St Paul's Cathedral in the background: all Wells' references to other capital cities were deleted.)

*A ruined room*: 'everything twelve years old and shabby and patched. (A thing to be noted in all these ruinous scenes is the dearth of china, glass and cutlery. I noted that such breakable gear was extremely short in Russia in 1920.)'

*The ruined Market Square*: 'Familiar skyline. Ragged people. Marketing. A peasant with a horse-drawn motor car.'

*John Cabal's aeroplane*: '... it is a plane of the 1930–40 type, but it roars cheerfully. ... A man appears in a modern (1975) flying kit, a shining black suit with a peculiar vizor that swings down upon his chest ... gas armour.'
(In the film the plane is also shiny, black and torpedo-like.)

*The Boss's Headquarters*: 'a vast desk in some large, partly ruined building (NB A broken-down telephone) ... So a barbarian chief with his captains and mistresses and ruffian courtiers might have sat amidst the ruins of an Imperial Roman City.'

*The Boss's fleet*: 'a strange miscellany of aeroplanes, most of them with a touch of Heath Robinson about them. (We want someone here who can make burlesque aeroplanes.)'
(In the film, the planes are beaten-up Avro 504s.)

*The Basra Bomber*: 'The air fight in this scene is not visible on the screen'; but one character helpfully notes, as he watches, 'It's less like an aeroplane than a flying fort.'
(In the film, the airfight *is* visible on the screen.)

*The transformation of Everytown*: '*A sequence of creative work and power.* Flashes to give a crescendo of strenuous activity to balance the first war crescendo ... work in furnaces, upon embankments, in mines, upon great plantations. Men working in laboratories. This will have to be drawn from contemporary stuff, but that stuff must be *futurised* by putting unfamiliar flying machines in the air, projecting giant machines in the foreground, making great discs and curved forms swing and rotate enigmatically before the spectator. A lot of this may be contrived by blending small figures of workers with vast moving models of strange design.
Flashes of molten metal running.
Flash of some dark liquid dripping slowly while a man in a peculiar gas mask watches it.
Emphasise by banners, streamers and inscriptions: RESEARCH INVENTION WORLD PLANNING AND SCIENTIFIC CONTROL.

There is a progressive improvement in the clothing of the workers and the neatness and vigour of the machinery as this series goes through. New architectural forms appear presently, prevail for a few flashes and pass. Compare the description of time-travelling in the TIME MACHINE.'

*Oswald Cabal's study*: 'He wears a white tunic, which has a broad yoke with which various gadgets are connected. He has a gauntlet [with gadgets] on his left arm and a small wristlet on his right – silk or metal shot or open-work trunk hose and light shoes. Modern fittings. The air is conditioned about him and the light perfect. It is a diffused light from the ceiling – no lamps. There are no windows and no hinged doors [no pillars or right-angle joints ... the window, with a glimpse of the city ways outside, has no frame but is merely a piece of transparent soundproof wall] ... No pictures and very little bric-a-brac.'

*The City Ways*: 'Moving platforms, spiral ways vanishing into tunnels, exposed lifts. Drifts of people come and go. A vision of the city interior of the new age. General impression here of architecture and structure.'

*Everytown in the year 2054*: 'The creative forces in mankind have triumphed and the face of the earth has changed. There is serenity and beauty in the scenery of this last part. .. The general effect is of a very beautiful, gentle hill country, agreeably wooded with a few groups of enigmatical buildings. The same characteristic skyline of hill that we have seen since the beginning of the film reappears ... No smoking ... Everything is pellucid and clean.'

(These sequences of 'serenity and beauty' – representing the final phase in *The Shape of Things to Come* – were to be conflated with the earlier sequences following the montage of 'creative work and power' in the film, so that the future world was eventually presented in only one historical period.)

*The Space Gun*: 'The gun is a vast mortar-like shell-within-shell gun. The Moon cylinder is a metallic cylinder $30 \times 10$ feet in diameter, poised above the gun. It looks very small in comparison with the concentric shell of the Space Gun. ... The general effect is one of *monstrous* structures upheld by a delicate lattice. ... Through the midst of this vast structural mass swirls a torrent of turbine water.'

(The film followed this description closely, except that the turbine

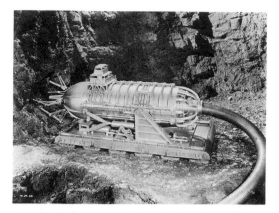

6 0    The transformation of Everytown: 'a sequence of creative work and power'

water was replaced by huge thrusters working on a 'gun bolt' principle.)

*Whither Mankind?*: 'Cabal and Passworthy [are] very still on a great enclosed platform above the city in starlight, not peeping through a telescope or tube of any sort, but watching a disc.'
(In the film, this 'disc' became a giant white reflector, with telescope in the background.)

The literature on *Things to Come* is unclear about who exactly was responsible for transforming these 'general effects' and 'general impression of architecture and structure' into the design of the finished film. Books about H. G. Wells attribute most of the best ideas to him; books about the history of film design tend to prefer William Cameron Menzies; articles about Vincent Korda assume that he made the final decisions; while a recent biography of Alexander Korda claims that the Hungarian artist-designer Laszlo Moholy-Nagy was 'hired . . . to design the sets'. Histories of design tend, understandably, to stress the Moholy factor – from Bauhaus to Wellshouse. On one thing all seem to be agreed, though: as Wells put it, 'Many of the sequences which slipped quite easily from my pen were extremely difficult to screen.'
    It seems to have happened like this. Having completed the treatment which included *his* design suggestions as we've seen, Wells made tentative approaches to Vincent Korda's friend Fernard Léger and asked him to supply concept sketches and costume ideas for the city of the future. Léger had designed the laboratory sequences for Marcel L'Herbier's *L'Inhumaine* (1924) – full of cut-out wheels, revolving discs, tubes, dials, spirals and pendulums, with lab assistants dressed in shiny black boilersuits – and the scenes in *Whither Mankind?* of Theotocopulos broadcasting to the world were partly based on the equivalent scenes in *L'Inhumaine* of the heartless diva broadcasting to listeners everywhere through a video contraption designed by the scientist/engineer Einar Norsen. But Wells found Léger's drawings (four weeks' work) too much like a kinetic backdrop, and too reminiscent of *Ballet Mécanique*, which had been filmed while *L'Inhumaine* was in production. So Le Corbusier – who in 1922 had designed a fantasy city for three million people with sixty-storey towers and aeroplanes flying around below roof level (despite the down-drafts, this had already become a cliché of

tomorrow's metropolis) – was approached instead. Wells was dead
against 'ultra skyscrapers', but thought that the high priest of the 'new
architecture' might supply some interesting solutions. Le Corbusier,
however, responded by saying that the people living in Wells' city of
2054 were far too old-fashioned in their attitudes, and far too 1934 in
their leisure activities. And he wasn't too excited by the idea of an
*underground* city either.

At this point Vincent Korda, in his son Michael's words, began

busily ransacking the libraries for avant-garde furniture designs,
architectural fantasies, helicopters and autogyros, monorails and
electric bubble cars, television sets and space vehicles. The
nursery in Hampstead became a repository for his rejected design
models, and while other children were playing with trains and toy
soldiers, I was playing with rocket ships, ray guns and flying
wings.

From Le Corbusier's *Vers une Architecture* (1927) he gleaned the ideas of
a geometrically laid out garden city – as seen through the frameless
windows of Oswald Cabal's office; of villas with suspended gardens,
and of a giant aircraft hangar – like the one being built in the
background of the Basra conference – constructed out of half-oval steel
hoops. The massed aeroplanes flying over the white cliffs of Dover, and
bird's eye views of Everytown, may well have come from collaged
photographs in Le Corbusier's *Aircraft (L'Avion)*, translated in 1935. An
architectural historian has recently written that 'although Le Corbusier
was known, and indeed notorious, to British architects ... in the 1930s,
this was mainly through his books'; so his contribution to the
development of British design was 'insignificant'. Vincent Korda's
explicit use of Le Corbusier's ideas in *Things to Come* would suggest that
his architectural language, if not his name, was after February 1936 far
better known in the *public* domain.

The Basra Bombers, with their twin fuselages and four propellers
apiece, probably came from the 'By air tomorrow' chapter of Norman
Bel Geddes' book *Horizons* (1932), where a drawing of the vast Air
Liner Number 4, 'a tailless "V"-winged monoplane carrying a total of
606 passengers [with] a total wing spread of 528 feet' and ten
propellers, was reproduced over four pages and described in

considerable detail. Also from *Horizons* may have come the city square of Everytown where Theotocopulos appears on a television screen (based on Bel Geddes' design for a modern amphitheatre) and aspects of Cabal's villa (based on Bel Geddes' aerial restaurant). The rounded, white Bakelite (?) tanks of the enemy in the Second World War resemble the 1932 streamlined ocean liner from the same book, with a touch of Ecko radio cabinets about them.

Where 'avant-garde furniture designs' were concerned, Vincent Korda had evidently looked closely at illustrations of the glass room designed by interior architect Oliver Hill for the Exhibition of British Industrial Art at the Dorland Hall in 1933: the room, which was full of bent glass items – a chair, stool, couch, bed and table – had achieved a certain notoriety in the press when Hill suggested that a nude model be posed on the glass couch as a publicity stunt, but was put off the idea when he was told the glass would probably shatter. But Vincent Korda's versions were not in fact made of glass: they were made of a less brittle new display plastic called Rhodoid which, according to an advertisement in the graphics magazine *Display* (December 1936), was available in 'rigid, polished, matt or embossed sheets'. The rooms and

Le Corbusier's garden city, as re-designed by Vincent Korda

staircases in which this furniture was displayed, in the film, resemble
the semicircular, cantilevered terraces facing the sea in the De la Warr
Pavilion, Bexhill – designed by Erich Mendelsohn and Serge
Chermayeff, and prominently in the architectural news in 1934. As for
the 'helicopters and … flying wings', Korda designed a white bubble-
like variation on the Asboth type of helicopter – for Oswald Cabal and
party to beat the rebels to the Space Gun – and placed a picture of a
Douglas Commercial mark 3 over John Cabal's mantelpiece: the
streamlined DC3 was introduced commercially in 1935 and, as Wells
had requested, emphasised Cabal's 'association with the airforce'. *Flight*
magazine (27 February 1936) reckoned that 'from the aeronautical
point of view, apart from any other, congratulations are due to those
responsible'.

The Space Gun itself was closely based on the instructions in the
treatment, and proved to be one of the more controversial aspects of the
film's design. It was soon pointed out by the *Journal of the British
Interplanetary Society* that the gun-fired projectile was 'based on an
outstanding misconception' because it would exert a force of about 435
tons on each of the astronauts and immediately reduce them to

The Basra Bombers, probably based on a design concept by Norman Bel Geddes

raspberry jam; no scientist had seriously considered the 'gun' idea of space travel 'since the days of Jules Verne' (*From the Earth to the Moon*). The dreaded Fritz Lang's *Woman in the Moon* (1929), last of the silent science fiction epics and the film which invented the idea of a sixty-second 'countdown' to enhance the tension, had already introduced the idea of an explosion-boosted rocket (courtesy of Professor Hermann Oberth, assisted by Wernher von Braun, who were the technical advisers), so there was even a cinematic precedent. The publicity people, quick to spot something the audience might laugh at, blotted out the Space Gun and redrew the posters to show a sleek rocket with fire coming out of its tail. But Wells had been adamant, and unusually detailed in his prescriptions: just as the Work sequence would 'balance the first war crescendo' – showing energies being channelled *productively* in the future – so the Space Gun would balance the destructive technology of the opening air-raid, with is smaller-scale anti-aircraft gun pointing towards the stars from Everytown Square. Surprisingly, the much-maligned Space Gun was to have a delayed impact on the design of the future: at the New York World's Fair of 1939, industrial designer Raymond Loewy produced a Rocketport for the Chrysler

pavilion which showed a New York to London passenger rocket being fired from a spiral cannon by means of 'compressed air'.

But it was the underground piazza of Everytown in 2036 which attracted most attention. In this interior space which looked like a gigantic white ribcage – representing both the 'city ways' *and* the 'architecture and structure' of Wells' treatment – Vincent Korda combined flying walkways, lifts in transparent ducts, curved balconies, ornamental trees growing on elevated terraces, all bathed in artificial light in a grandiose fusion of Le Corbusier and American streamlining. Which is to say a fusion of European and American Modernism. Much of this was made possible by the American 'special effects director' Ned Mann (who had worked with Cameron Menzies on *The Thief of Bagdad*): he combined the life-sized lower levels of buildings for people to walk around with miniatures of the upper levels reaching towards the surface of the earth, as well as images of crowds projected onto tiny screens within miniatures, and models of people moving on belts towards the Space Gun; and he was assisted in this by trainee Wally Veevers, who much later went on to become one of the key Special Effects Supervisors, with Douglas Trumbull, on *2001: A Space Odyssey*. This special effects work at Isleworth made Everytown 2036 possible; but it also, unfortunately, created precisely the opposite impression to the one Wells had been hoping for when he wrote that the people of the future 'are individualised workers doing responsible co-operative team work'. It created the impression of individual *heroes* lording it over the tiny ants who massed below them – a message which mightily depressed the Fabians Beatrice and Sidney Webb, who went into Farnham to see the film in November 1936:

> The human home of future ages is to be without an outlook on the beauties of nature. ... Within masses of moving machinery, multitudes of men and women and children scurrying about like ants in a broken open ant hill: they seem moved by herd impulse not by individual minds. Restless, intolerably restless, is this new society of men: ugly and depressing in its sum total.

Today, the underground piazza seems to prophesy the huge American superhotels designed by architect and developer John Portman in the late 1960s, or perhaps a shopping mall or the terminal of an international airport. At the time, the design press was sufficiently impressed to devote a lot of space to this aspect of *Things to Come*. Modernism in Hollywood movies had until then been synonymous with upward mobility, fast bucks and some of the most memorable seductions (often involving Greta Garbo) in the history of cinema. Warner Bros gangsters may have started life as dead-end kids, but once they had made it the scene would shift to the 'moderne' office above the equally 'moderne' speakeasy, with a Cubist painting on the wall; the more established goodies, by contrast, tended to prefer vernacular interiors with sporting prints over the fireplace. Hollywood moguls, many of whom started life in the fashion business, had done a lot to popularise Modernism (or the International Style, as it was known in America), but had jettisoned all the social theory – to put it mildly – in the process. *Things to Come* was defiantly Modernist – in its analysis of the future *as well as* its look – and therefore deserved to be taken more seriously. It was released in Britain at a time when a small group of English activists was busy trying to promote the tenets of the European Modern Movement in architecture to a public which found them highly resistible: W. Heath Robinson's *How to Live in a Flat* (1936), which satirised their missionary zeal, was proving particularly popular. 'Whereas formerly the best furniture was made by carpenters, cabinet-makers and similar skilled craftsmen', wrote Heath Robinson and his co-author K. R. G. Browne, 'nowadays the trade is almost entirely in the hands of plumbers, riveters, blow-pipers and metal-workers of all sorts. As a result the ultra-modern living room resembles a cross between an operating-theatre, a dipsomaniac's nightmare and a new kind of knitting.'

*The Architectural Review*, a journal which was deeply committed to Modernism in the mid-1930s, was usually sniffy about the design of Hollywood movies, but in February 1936 it included a double-page spread of the sets from *Things to Come* together with the thought that the 'Light Architecture in the subterranean city mechanically constructed by the post-war generation' was a very 'encouraging' sign of how film functionalism had moved on since *Metropolis* and was 'easily the best work of its kind yet done in England'. The April issue included a still of Everytown in an article about Le Corbusier's contribution to town planning. The less committed *Architects' Journal* (27 February 1936) was also less convinced.

From the architectural point of view, somebody must have had a lot of fun adapting from ... Norman Bel Geddes and one or two others: the result occasionally showing the applied art which we are all supposed to dislike so much nowadays. And I am quite convinced that I saw Mr Oliver Hill's famous glass bed still in active use in about A.D. 2070. Or was the owner a collector of antiques? ... [But] *Things to Come* is a good film which very definitely ought to be seen by architects

The issue of a month before had featured two full-page stills, with captions about the challenging idea of a 'whole city roofed in, with traffic circulations at various levels'. *Design for Today* (April 1936), published by the Design and Industries Association, found in a long feature that the shattering of the contemporary world in early sequences was much more convincing than the 'reproduction of a futuristic world': the abiding impression of 'the Wells–Korda world of 2036 A.D.' was of 'showiness and an over-dependence on mere size'. But where *Design for Today* really took issue with *Things to Come* was over the unfortunate image of the designer contained in the film – an image which had evidently unsettled the Association, pledged to raising the profile of the profession:

> Of all the characters, perhaps the most crudely imagined is the Artist-type, Theotocopulos (why a Greek name?); who, when first seen, is nibbling splinters of stone from the side of a colossal statue, not remarkably well-proportioned, and for some reason resembling a sixth-century Attic goddess. Here is the Artist-Reactionary, the villain of the piece: someone whose work is not merely devoid of utility (as against that of the scientist) but entirely imitative. *Wells, it appears, does not conceive of the designer or the architect – inevitably first-order forces in his future world – as in any sense artists.* Yet this silly little man, with his unwieldy Pallas, is in reality not an artist at all – much less the Artist as a type.

Besides, the article added waspishly, 'the glass couch somehow reminds one of Burlington House' (where an exhibition of 'British Art in Industry', much criticised by the design establishment, had featured an Oliver Hill bathroom and bedroom in 1935). *Decoration* (March 1936) noted that some critics 'have objected to the clothes and decoration of 2030 as portrayed in the film', and promised a lead article to redress the balance in the April issue. In this article, which was lavishly illustrated, S. John Woods thundered back at the carpers:

> The last three and a half reels are at once the most damning comment *on the present* and the most stimulating illustration of what would be possible *in the present*, here and now in 1936 not in 2036, if only the world were seized from Profit and run by Sanity. Utopia, idealistic, dreams, you say. So what? ... The criticism that the design of the 2036 environment is really 1936 is irrelevant. Korda–Wells – etc. have surveyed the contemporary world, its architecture, interior decoration, and the thousand other factors which contribute their quota towards environment, they have discovered the highest common denominator and carried the equation a stage further. The solution? Space, light and precision. ... White and glass may be out of fashion at the moment, but they will return if the problem which closes *Things to Come* is answered as it should be answered. For that, and to see the capabilities of 1936, go to *Things to Come* if you have not already done so.

By showing the effect of 'things *planned* instead of *happening*', the film had done a great service to the International Modern aesthetic. It was an aesthetic shared by Rebecca West, no less, who had written for the same magazine in 1934 (issue 4): 'Till the modernists got working the English house was not only stately, it was soup-coloured. It was dark, muddy and congested. I claim for the modern decorator that he has *washed the public eye* ... design should be coherent and colours should be clean.'

Outside the design world, newspapers were fairly evenly divided as to the merits of Everytown 2036. Graham Greene, in the *Spectator* (28 February 1936), thought the first third of the film was 'magnificent' but judged the 'vision of the world peopled by beautiful idealistic scientists' to be sentimental and strangely old-fashioned. *The Times* (21 February) thought 'the new world, with all its machinery and vistas of glass and steel, is so large and glittering, and so obviously a working model, that one cannot imagine how it could have been done.' Alistair Cooke, in the *Listener* (18 March) – the best-known review of the film, today –

reckoned that 'it must be heartbreaking for Mr Wells to be told that the costumes he predicted they'd be wearing in 2030 are to be the very thing in beach-wear this summer. ... *Things to Come* shares with most Utopias the primary error of making today the premiss.' But he did concede that 'Vincent Korda is the hero of the piece. ... When it comes to considering what sort of rooms we shall be living in in forty years (mine's in oak, just six feet by three) your guess is as good as mine. But it could hardly be as good as Vincent Korda's. By a few imaginative strokes on his drawing board he has made the piece a lovely thing to look at.' The costumes to which Alistair Cooke referred – unisex wide-shouldered samurai outfits, with matching white mini-skirts, bare legs and sandals – were to have been designed by Léger, but in the end were entrusted to the young English painter John Armstrong, assisted by the Marchioness of Queensberry (who, as Cathleen Mann, was shortly to produce a lorry-bill informing motorists that 'Film Stars use Shell', complete with an image of a Madonna clutching a seashell, lit by Futurist searchlights and with a face resembling an etched glass Deco sculpture). Wells liked the idea of costumes incorporating 'light apparatus' (the body as machine, another prophetic thought), and enjoyed the samurai reference since it fitted his image of an elite group, but had been worried that the people of the future might too much resemble 'super-sandwich men'.

C. A. Lejeune, in the *Observer* (23 February), was even more convinced about Everytown 2036 than Alistair Cooke: 'There has never been anything in the cinema like *Things to Come*. No film, not even *Metropolis*, has even slightly resembled it. ... The film has been used for the first time to state a hard and fairly complex argument, and to state it with a force and beauty that gives you no choice but to follow and attend.' Sydney W. Carroll, in the *Sunday Times* (same day), agreed: he called the film 'a stupendous spectacle, an overwhelming Doréan, Jules Vernesque, elaborated *Metropolis*, staggering to the eye, mind and spirit'.

These design ideas were derived by Vincent Korda from Wells' treatment, in discussion with William Cameron Menzies (who himself designed elements of the 'war' sequences, including the 'huge shadowgraph phantoms' of soldiers marching behind Passworthy's young son) and Ned Mann. Some models and drawings – especially for the miniature machines, noisy streamlined vacuum cleaner and silent dispenser of prefabricated walls, in the Work sequence – were provided by Frank Wells. Together, they came up with the nice idea of bombing a *cinema* – which advertises *Lucretia Borgia*, an Alexander Korda production manqué, in moderne lettering recently designed by Walter Dorwin Teague – in the first reel. So, what was the contribution of the former *Bauhausler* Laszlo Moholy-Nagy, who has been called the man who 'designed the sets' but whose sets are said to have been 'too far ahead of their time' and thus rejected?

Moholy-Nagy settled in London, initially at Lawn Road Flats, Hampstead, in May 1935. He had been invited over by the recently formed Modern Architectural Research Group, and was a refugee from the Nazis, who had closed the Bauhaus (where Moholy was a 'form master' in the 1920s). Vincent Korda had known him since 1930, and his brother Alexander had worked with him in Hungary as early as 1917. As a calling card, Moholy showed his short film *Light-play* (1930) to the Kordas and Ned Mann at London Films, and Vincent Korda asked him to develop it into a sequence of visual ideas for the five-and-a-half-minute Work sequence, showing the rebuilding of Everytown. At this stage, Korda himself had very ambitious ideas for the sequence – from black and white into colour, from the standard ratio to a wider screen – and thought he might be able to integrate these with Moholy's effects. So Moholy-Nagy set to work at Worton Hall studios (*not* at home, as most of the books claim) with trainee trick photography assistant Wally Veevers. In an interview with Terence Senter, Veevers was to recall that Moholy was 'then creating and shooting a montage sequence of futuristic effects, using various coiled glass tubing, bottles, bubbling liquids, back light effects and smoke, etc., to achieve his aim', between early November and mid-December 1935. Bliss's music had already been recorded, so the length and pace were set, and there was plenty of Rhodoid lying around – which excited him a lot. According to Sibyl Moholy-Nagy, the basic idea, building on *Light-play* and derived from Russian Constructivist sculpture, was to 'eliminate solid form. Houses were no longer obstacles to, but receptacles of, man's natural life force, light. There were no walls, but skeletons of steel, screened with glass and plastic sheets. The accent was on perforation and contour, an *indication* of a new reality rather than reality itself.'

Since Moholy had written, in his collaged book *Von Material zu Architektur*, that 'we need Utopians of genius, a new Jules Verne: not to sketch in broad perspective an easily grasped technical utopia but the very *existence* of future men', he was evidently in his element. H. G. Wells had been something of a hero to the Futurists when they designed their fantasy cities just before the First World War, and it is likely that he was known to Moholy as well: certainly, the theme of the central role of technology in the world of the future appealed strongly to him. Stills of these researches for *Things to Come* have survived, and in autumn 1975 film researcher Lisa Pontecorvo discovered four discarded shots on 35 mm in the Movietone News Library, Denham, while preparing an Open University documentary on *Moholy-Nagy – painting, photography, film.* Some of them filmed through a multiplying prism, they show an explosion of light, transparent revolving cones surrounded by miniature cantilevered buildings (resembling Mies van der Rohe's glass skyscraper concepts of 1922), rectangular sheets of punched Rhodoid moving in a line like suspended curtain windows, and a glass ball with oil bubbles against a grid background.

When Moholy-Nagy saw the finished sequence in *Things to Come*, he was 'bitterly disappointed': only some ninety seconds of his work had survived, intercut in 'flashes' with the designs of Korda, Mann and Frank Wells and with found footage of industrial turbines. He particularly missed the revolving cones and see-through cantilevered buildings, which he reckoned had been dropped through 'editorial timidity'. According to Vincent Korda, the shots which survived included: bent glass tubes filled with mercury; a latticed plane which explodes into light particles; a sparkling bowl, seen through strips of Rhodoid with a tablespoon behind it; spinning rollers and a revolving spiral; illuminated glass tubes in bubbling liquid; a meter with numbers; a diver in a helmet seen through corrugated glass; and the visual idea (derived from Wells) of a tiny technician looking after a huge generator. Moholy was later to publish stills from his researches – such as the diver behind corrugated glass – in American Bauhaus brochures and articles, and he exhibited some of his footage separately. Perhaps as a consolation prize, Alexander Korda agreed to finance a short Moholy-Nagy film in 1936, released two years later as *Lobsters*.

The experiment of using a distinguished Bauhaus designer to contribute to the Modernist vision of Everytown – on the face of it, a marriage made in heaven – had not been a success. Avant-garde films about the play of light did not, it seemed, blend easily with the demands

7 4    Laszlo Moholy-Nagy's visual ideas for the 'rebuilding of Everytown' sequence

of big-budget film-making. In July 1937, Moholy-Nagy joined his colleague and closest friend Walter Gropius in America, to direct the short-lived new Bauhaus in Chicago and, in 1938, found his own School of Design there. H. G. Wells, in his private diary, makes no mention of him.

But Wells did have plenty to say about the design of the film. He, too, had had high hopes in 1935, but this was followed by 'disillusionment later, 1936'. In retrospect he saw the visualisation of his treatment as 'pretentious, clumsy and scamped': 'I grew tired of writing stuff into the treatment that was afterwards mishandled ... in the end little more of *The Shape of Things to Come* was got over than a spectacular suggestion of a Cosmopolis ruled by men of science and affairs.' The film's 'noisy heaviness would damage my prestige, perhaps irreparably'. By way of revenge perhaps, he wrote a long short story in 1936–7 called *Star Begotten – a biological fantasia*, about the effect of cosmic rays from Mars as earthly geniuses. As part of the extensive dialogue, he had one of his characters bitterly admit:

> World peace is assumed, but the atmosphere of security simply makes [the people of the future] rather aimless, fattish and out of training. They are collectively up to nothing – or they are off in a storm of collective hysteria to conquer the moon or some remote nonsense like that. Imaginative starvation. They have apparently made no advances whatever in subtlety, delicacy, simplicity. Rather the reverse. They never say a witty thing; they never do a charming act. The general effect is of very pink, rather absurdly dressed celluloid dolls living on tabloids in a glass lavatory.

H. G. Wells had discovered, at the age of seventy, that the business of film-making was not for him. 'I was taken by surprise,' he concluded, 'by difficulties I should have foreseen.' The public would now think of him as a mere technophiliac. If only he had managed to communicate what was so clearly in *his* mind to Korda's people.

## POSTSCRIPT: WHICH SHALL IT BE?

Although 1936 was the year of London Transport's Constructivist air-brushed poster 'By Bus to the Pictures Tonight', not too many people seem to have gone by bus to see *Things to Come*. It was a critical success, but only did moderately well at the box-office. Alexander Korda tried to put a brave face on things: when asked if the film would ever break even, he would reply, 'Of course. It was an expensive effort but we're only a few thousands out at the moment.' An American film distributor was more blunt about it. 'Nobody is going to believe,' he said, 'that the world is going to be saved by a bunch of people with British accents.' Perhaps, in Britain, the scenes of aerial bombardment were found to be *too* upsetting; or perhaps word had got around about the preachiness of the piece; or perhaps Wells was on the wane; or perhaps it was that Space Gun.

Disturbing stills from the blitz sequence were subsequently published in a book called *Aerial Wonders of Our Time*, which warned the government and anyone else who might be listening of the imminent danger of 'death from the skies'. When *Things to Come* was reissued as a

The devastating effects of the air raid on Everytown

second feature, in suburban cinemas, in 1940, Mass Observation reporters noted that the shots of squadron after squadron of enemy planes flying unharmed over the white cliffs of Dover were greeted with laughter, but that the sequence of panic in the streets following the air-raid were watched in complete silence. The anti-war discussions in John Cabal's house also 'aroused interest'. One witness reckoned that in retrospect the film had proved to be 'a provoking prophecy'.

Various cuts had been made, at the end of post-production. The release script includes several scenes and passages of dialogue – Passworthy on war, John Cabal chatting to Dr Harding about the Boss, a rabble-rousing banqueting scene in the Boss's headquarters, the long discussion between Roxana and Mary about gender roles, a lesson about improvements in health under the New World Order and about the engineering of the Space Gun, some of Theotocopulos's televised speech, a conversation between Cabal, Passworthy and their children – which were filmed but pruned at the last minute. The print shown at the trade show was, according to Rachael Low, 9,781 feet or 108.67 minutes; the *Monthly Film Bulletin* noted its running time as 108 minutes. The release print was 98 minutes, so between trade and premiere there had been cuts of ten minutes. Mysteriously, most of today's film guides (following Halliwell) list the original running time as 113 minutes; some go as high as 130 minutes. But there is no evidence that a version longer than 108 minutes was ever publicly screened. Video versions tend to run about 95 minutes – which, allowing for different speeds, translates as the original 98 minutes in the cinema.

Wells' published and novelised shooting-script – *Things to Come – a film story ... based on The Shape of Things to Come* – includes many sequences which were either abandoned once filming had started or cut before the trade show. The novelisation was written in summer 1935, when the film was still to be called *Whither Mankind?* The abandoned or cut sequences included: a much longer children's party in which the main character 'types' are revealed as youngsters; detail and comment about the activities of Wadsky the 'Oriental' profiteer which – mercifully – were cut to a minimum in the finished film; more developed relationships between John Cabal, Roxana and Mary Harding; scenes among the 'city ways' of Everytown in 2055 (including an Athletic Club) with a short digression on eugenics; the character of Oswald Cabal's estranged wife Rowena – who is the 'descendant of

7 8    Rowena (Margaretta Scott) enters a 2036 interior – in a sequence cut from the final print

Roxana', is played by the same actress, Margaretta Scott, and takes up the discussion of gender roles and family life where her predecessor left off – who *was* filmed, to judge by many surviving stills and indeed the credit titles; the broadcasting of Theotocopulos's speech to a varied 'world audience', which leads on to – among many other things – a discussion about Pavlov's contribution to 'canine genetics' and the entrance of a 'very intelligent-looking dog' who 'can almost talk and will never have distemper'; much more detailed treatment of Theotocopulos's demonstration in the city and at the Space Gun, accompanied by a rousing insurrectionary song; the effects of the blast-off on the demonstrators, who are 'caught in the whirlwind' while their leader struggles 'ridiculously in his own cloak'. The demonstrators are *not* killed, as some commentators have written: they are just made to look foolish. So there could well have been a 113-minute version at one time, and it is likely that the rough cut was considerably longer. H. G. Wells certainly felt sore about the fact that 'they had to cut out a good half of my dramatic scenes' in the last third of the film.

But by 1940, when the film was re-released to cash in on the fact that it had predicted the outbreak of the Second World War and the blitz, Wells had adjusted to the fact that, despite his age, he was 'still learning, still growing'. Poison gas hadn't been used yet, but it might be. Observing the events in Europe of 1939–40, he wrote bitterly: 'God damn you all. I told you so.'

# CREDITS

. . . . . . . . . . . . . . . . . . . . . . . .

## Things to Come

**GB**
1936
**Production company**
London Film Productions
**GB premiere**
21 February 1936
**US premiere**
17 April 1936
**Distributor**
United Artists
**Producer**
Alexander Korda
**Production manager**
David B. Cunynghame
**Director**
William Cameron Menzies
**Assistant director**
Geoffrey Boothby
**Screenplay**
H. G. Wells from his novel
*The Shape of Things to Come*;
assisted by Lajos Biró
(uncredited)
**Photography (black and
white)**
Georges Périnal
**Camera operator**
Robert Krasker
**2nd camera operator**
Bernard Browne
**Music**
Arthur Bliss
**Music director**
Muir Mathieson
**Supervising editor**
William Hornbeck
**Editors**
Charles Crichton,
Francis Lyon
**Settings designer**
Vincent Korda
**Assistant art director**
Frank Wells
**Associate art directors**
(uncredited) John Bryan,
William Cameron Menzies,
Frederick Pusey

**Costume designers**
John Armstrong, René
Hubert, The Marchioness of
Queensberry
**Special effects director**
Ned Mann
**Special effects
photography**
Edward Cohen
**Assistant special effects**
Lawrence Butler
**Trick photography**
(uncredited) Harry Zech,
Wally Veevers, Ross Jacklin
**Visual consultant, Work
sequence**
(uncredited) Laszlo Moholy-
Nagy
**Aeronautical adviser**
Nigel Tangye

**Raymond Massey**
*John Cabal/Oswald Cabal*
**Edward Chapman**
*Pippa Passworthy/Raymond
Passworthy*
**Ralph Richardson**
*The Boss*
**Margaretta Scott**
*Roxana/Rowena*
**Cedric Hardwicke**
*Theotocopulos*
**Maurice Braddell**
*Dr Harding*
**Sophie Stewart**
*Mrs Cabal*
**Derrick De Marney**
*Richard Gordon*
**Ann Todd**
*Mary Gordon*
**Pearl Argyle**
*Catherine Cabal*
**Kenneth Villiers**
*Maurice Passworthy*
**Ivan Brandt**
*Morden Mitani*
**Anne McLaren**
*The child*

**Patricia Hilliard**
*Janet Gordon*
**Charles Carson**
*Great-grandfather*

and (uncredited)
**Allan Jeayes**
*Grandfather Cabal*
**Pickles Livingstone**
*Horrie Passworthy*
**Anthony Holles**
*Simon Burton*
**John Clements**
*German fighter pilot*
**Abraham Sofaer**
*Wadsky*
**Patrick Barr**
*World Transport official*
**George Sanders**
*Pilot*
**Paul O'Brien**

Credits checked by Markku
Salmi.
The print of *Things to Come*
in the National Film and
Television Archive derives
from material acquired from
London Films.

A film called *H. G. Wells's
The Shape of Things to Come*
(directed by George
McGowan) was released in
1979. Despite the title, and a
character called 'Dr. John
Caball' (Barry Morse), this
garish mix of *Star Trek* and
*Star Wars* – depicting life on
the Moon Colony of 'New
Washington', after the great
robot wars masterminded by
the evil Omus from the
planet Delta 3 (Jack
Palance) – bears no
resemblance either to
Wells's book or to the film
*Things to Come*.

# SELECT BIBLIOGRAPHY

## a) Things to Come

BFI microfilm dossier of reviews and press-books
Cedric Hardwicke: *A Victorian in Orbit* (New York: Doubleday, 1961)
Raymond Massey: *A hundred different lives* (London: Robson, 1979)
Garry O'Connor: *Ralph Richardson* (London: Hodder & Stoughton, 1982)
*Leon Stover: *The Prophetic Soul – a reading of H. G. Wells's Things to Come* (Jefferson, N. C.: McFarland, 1987)
*H. G. Wells: *Things to Come – a film story* (London: Cresset Press, 1935)

Items marked with * proved especially useful.

## b) Film Design

*Donald Albrecht: *Designing Dreams* (London: Thames & Hudson, 1987)
Leon Barsacq: *Caligari's Cabinet* (New York: New American Library, 1978)
Edward Carrick: *Art and Design in the British Film* (London: Dobson, 1948)
Edward Carrick: *The Influence of the Graphic Artist on Film* (J.R.S.A., March 1950)
Mary Corliss and Carlos Clarens: *Designed for Film, Film Comment*, May 1978
Christopher Frayling: *Grand Illusions, Blueprint*, Spring 1987
*Ezra Goodman: *The fifty year decline and fall of Hollywood* (New York: Simon & Schuster, 1961)
*John Hambley and Patrick Downing: *The Art of Hollywood* (London: Victoria & Albert Museum, 1979)
Beverly Heisner: *Hollywood Art* (North Carolina: Mcfarland, 1990)
*Harold Koszarski: *Hollywood Directors, 1914–40* (New York: Mcfarland, 1976)
Howard Mandelbaum and Eric Myers: *Screen Deco* (Bromley: Columbus Books, 1985)
*R. Myerscough-Walker: *Stage & Film Decor* (London: Pitman, 1939)
Robert Sennett: *Setting the Scene* (New York: Harry N. Abrams, 1994)

and *Film Dope* 42 (on Menzies)

## c) Design

Martin Battersby: *The Decorative Thirties* (London: Studio Vista, 1971)
*Norman Bel Geddes: *Horizons* (Boston: Little, Brown, 1932)
David Dean: *The Thirties – Recalling the English Architectural Scene* (London: Trefoil, 1983)
Jennifer Hawkins and Marianne Hollis (ed): *Thirties* (London: Arts Council of Great Britain, 1979)
A. Jackson: *The Politics of Architecture – a history of modern architecture in Britain* (London: Architectural Press, 1970)
Paul Jodard: *Raymond Loewy* (London: Trefoil, 1992)
Richard Kostelanetz (ed): *Moholy-Nagy* (London: Allen Lane, 1971)
*Le Corbusier: *Vers Une Architecture* (Paris: Editions Vincent, 1958)
Le Corbusier: *Aircraft* (London: Trefoil, 1987)
Ozenfant: *Foundations of Modern Art* (London: John Rodker, 1931)
*Alan Powers: *Oliver Hill* (London: Mouton Publications, 1989)
ed Michael Raeburn and Victoria Wilson: *Le Corbusier, architect of the century* (London: Arts Council of Great Britain, 1987)
Terence Senter: *Moholy-Nagy's English Photography, Burlington Magazine*, November 1981

Terence Senter (ed): *L. Moholy-Nagy* (London: Arts Council of Great Britain, 1980)
*Sibyl Moholy-Nagy: Experiment in Totality* (M.I.T. Press, 1969)

and *Architects Journal, Architectural Review, Decoration, Design for Today, Display, Flight, The Studio* for February–December 1936

## d) The Kordas

Alexander Korda: *British film – today and tomorrow in Footnotes to the Film*, ed. Davy, (London: Lovat Dickson, 1937)
*Michael Korda: *Charmed Lives* (New York: Random House, 1979)
Vincent Korda: *The Artist and the Film, Sight & Sound*, Spring 1934
*Karol Kulik: *Alexander Korda* (London: W. H. Allen, 1975)
Martin Stockham: *The Korda Collection* (London: Boxtree, 1992)
*Catherine Surowiec: *Accent on Design – four European art directors* (London: BFI, 1992)
Paul Tabori: *Alexander Korda – a biography* (London: Oldbourne, 1959)

and *Film Dope* 31 on all the Kordas

## e) H. G. Wells

I. F. Clarke: *Voices Prophesying War* (London: Oxford University Press, 1966)
*Michael Coren: *The Invisible Man* (London: Bloomsbury, 1993)
Harry Geduld (ed): *Authors on Film* (Bloomington: Indiana University Press, 1972)
Burt Goldblatt and Chris Steinbrunner: *Cinema of the Fantastic* (New York: Saturday Review Press, 1972)
*J. R. Hammond (ed): An *H. G. Wells Companion* (London: Macmillan, 1979)
(ed) W. Johnson: *Focus on the Science Fiction Film* (New Jersey: Prentice Hall, 1972)
*N. and J. Mackenzie: *The Time Traveller* (London: Weidenfeld, 1973)
P. Parrinder and C. Rolfe (ed): *H. G. Wells Under Revision* (London & Toronto: Associated University Press, 1990)
Thomas Renzi: *H. G. Wells – six scientific romances* (New Jersey: Scarecrow, 1992)
David C. Smith: *H. G. Wells – desperately mortal* (New York: Yale University Press, 1986)
W. W. Wager: *H. G. Wells and the World State* (New York: Yale University Press, 1961)
*G. P. Wells (ed): H. G. Wells in Love (London: Faber, 1984)
*H. G. Wells: Experiment in autobiography* vol 2,

(London: Gollancz & Cresset, 1934)
H. G. Wells: *Rules of Thumb for Things to Come, New York Times*, 12 April 1936
*H. G. Wells: *The Shape of Things to Come* (London: Everyman, 1993)
H. G. Wells: *Whither Britain?*, BBC Radio broadcast 9/1/34
*H. G. Wells: *The Work, Wealth and Happiness of Mankind* 2 vols, (London: Heinemann, 1932)
Anthony West: *H. G. Wells – aspects of a life* (London: Hutchinson, 1984)
Alan Wykes: *H. G. Wells and the Cinema* (London: Jupiter, 1977)

## f) Arthur Bliss

Arthur Bliss: *As I Remember* (London: Faber, 1970)
*Gregory Roscow (ed): *Bliss on Music* (Oxford: Oxford University Press, 1991)

and *Film Dope* 4 & 5

# ALSO PUBLISHED

If you would like further information about future BFI Film Classics or about other books on film, media and popular culture from BFI Publishing, please write to:

BFI Film Classics
British Film Institute
21 Stephen Street
London
W1P 2LN